THE
ULTIMATE
PAPER
AIRPLANE

by Richard Kline

Illustrations by Floyd Fogleman
and Richard Kline

A FIRESIDE BOOK
Published by Simon & Schuster, Inc.
New York

Copyright © 1985 by Richard Kline and Floyd Fogleman

First Fireside Edition, 1986, Published by Simon & Schuster, Inc.

1230 Avenue of the Americas, New York, New York 10020
FIRESIDE and colophon are registered trademarks of
Simon & Schuster, Inc.

Designed by
Manufactured in the United States of America

20 19 18 17

Library of Congress Cataloging in Publication Data

ISBN: 0-671-55551-0

"Smilin' Jack" cartoon on page 20 © 1936, Tribune Media Services

Illustrations on pp. 16. 26, and 56 used courtesy
of The Bettmann Archive

To Walter Mitty, without whose continuing inspiration
this undertaking would never have gotten off the ground.
And to my wife, Fran Bourdon,
who kept both of my feet firmly anchored in reality.

—Richard Kline

To my wife, Margaret, and to my two children,
Penny and Scott. Their love, patience and understanding
have helped make this project much easier.

—Floyd Fogleman

Acknowledgments

Since the Kline-Fogleman airfoil began its journey on a kitchen table and has since soared over Manhattan, through the U.S. Patent Office, and in and out of various laboratories, offices, and studios toward a still-uncertain destination, it is appropriate to acknowledge all those people and institutions who advertently, or inadvertently, helped it along the way.

Thank you to:
Warren Buchanan, Dr. John Nicolaides, Notre Dame's Athletic and Convocation Center along with its wind and smoke tunnels, Dick Cozzi, Orin Severin, Bill Churchill, the Academy of Aeronautics, Fred Lamparter, Ann Downes, Audrey Ball of *Time* magazine, Morley Safer, Don Hewlett, Igor Organesoff, Bill Wagner and CBS's "60 Minutes," Max Wild, Barry Adelman, Howard Singer, Ralph Bucknam, Martin Goldstein, Julius Fisher, Bill Wardlow, Mike Douglas, "Captain Kangaroo," "Wonderama," Dennis Marks, Bob McCallister, Al Wegner, Martin Scherer, Cy Preston, Marsha Potash, Gurney Williams, Scot Morris and *Omni* magazine, David Letterman, Diane Sawyer and Bill Kurtis of the "CBS Morning News," Regis Philbin of the ABC "Morning Show," Pete Reed, George Leu, Dan Santich, Dennis Donahue, Richard Foch, Gregory Tyler, Dan McConaughy, David Silwa, Jeremy Harris, Bill Drier and the U.S. Patent Office.

Special thanks go to Charles Wiesehahn for his photographs of the seven models of the Ultimate Paper Airplane.

Contents

CHAPTER SEVEN
How *Do* Airplanes Fly?
- 57 -

CHAPTER EIGHT
The Concept Explained
- 63 -

CHAPTER NINE
The Ultimate Paper Airplane
- 67 -

Patterns for the Ultimate Paper Airplane
- 91 -

THE
ULTIMATE
PAPER
AIRPLANE

CHAPTER ONE

First Impressions of Flight

On May 6, 1937, up in North Newington, Connecticut, Richard Kline was in the kitchen of the house where he lived. Suddenly, he heard his mother call from the yard with great excitement. "Dickie, come here. Quick!" He raced out the backdoor and down the steps into the yard. Looking straight up into the sky where his mother was pointing, he saw a giant spaceship hovering directly overhead. It was so enormous that it filled practically the entire sky. What was it? Aliens from another planet? The end of the world? As he watched in awe, he heard a slight hum coming from four tiny motors on the underside of the gigantic airship. Moving majestically, it was headed in the direction of the school where he attended first grade. Later, he would learn that he had seen the Hindenburg, *flying from Germany to Lakehurst, New Jersey. Before the day was over, it would vanish from the sky forever.*

Man has always had a fascination with flight. To leave the ground and move freely about in the air was something he just had to learn how to do. Perhaps it was a psychological need to escape from down-to-earth problems. After all, when you are in flight, your mind is totally absorbed in the experience. There is no time to dwell on the past or worry about the future. Everything is happening right now. This moment. But even suspended in the air, you are never completely free. There are forces of nature that must be utilized, others that must be defied. Men made many brave as well as foolish attempts to achieve what was long believed to be impossible. Yet, in spite of all the obstacles, flight was eventually accomplished in what we now realize was a relatively short time.

Leonardo da Vinci was perhaps one of the first to fold and fly a paper airplane. When he died in 1519, he left behind a wealth of ideas and inventions that were later to amaze the world by their diversity. Both an artist and a scientist, he tried to understand the rudiments of flight by studying the structure and movements of birds' wings. He was also the first to invent a parachute, at least on paper.

The earliest successful flights were made in hot-air balloons in late 1783 by the Montgolfier brothers, Joseph and Etienne, who became the toast of Paris. But the problem with the balloon was that you had very little control over your position and the direction in which you could travel. You could make the balloon go up and you could bring it down, but the rest depended on the wind.

According to many historians, it was Sir George Cayley, a Yorkshire baronet, who devised the first true airplane in 1804. It was a five-foot glider with a kite for wings totaling 200 square feet in area. But it took another several years before he was able to construct a full-sized version. And the first person actually to fly this experimental craft was a ten-year-old boy whom Cayley talked into being the pilot. This first manned flight was "several yards" down a hill. The three-wheeled flying glider was appropriately propelled by a push from the inventor.

Still the problem remained. A glider would go up—and it would certainly come down. But how to get an airplane to *stay up* and travel in the direction you wanted to go?

In 1900, Wilbur and Orville Wright approached the problem by building a large kite, a full-sized, tailless, two-winged glider big enough to carry a man. Through careful study of the glider's reactions to strong sea breezes off the coast of Kitty Hawk, North Carolina, they learned that they could control the glider in flight by altering the shape of the wings, and they devised a system whereby the pilot could give the wings an upward twist on one side and downward twist on the other by means of wires attached to levers directly in front of him. But it was still a glider, at the mercy of the wind, and the Wright brothers realized that they needed a power plant on board that would create its own wind to lift the craft into the air and keep it aloft. However, no engine existed at that time that could meet their specifications, nor could they interest anyone in building one.

Wilbur and Orville owned a shop in Dayton, Ohio, where they designed, manufactured, and repaired bicycles. In their line of work they had acquired a great deal of knowledge about engineering and had even built a gasoline-powered motor to run a lathe and drill press at their shop. They designed and built their own aircraft engine in just six weeks, and on December 17, 1903, they made their first successful powered flight. Finally, an aircraft had been invented that was capable of flying *through* the air rather than riding on it.

It is difficult to relate today's sleek supersonic planes to that first fragile craft that took off and flew 122 feet over the sandy, wind-swept beach at Kitty Hawk. But we have learned that Leonardo was not wrong to study the structure and movements of birds' wings. For the shape of the wings of a plane, like the shape of a bird's wing, is critical to its flight. If God had meant us to fly, so the old saying went, we would have been born with wings. We were not. But we were born with brains.

Like many small boys, I was intrigued by airplanes. Zooming around the backyard, arms outstretched, growling in imitation of an engine, I *was* an airplane. But, growing up, such was my nature that I never had any desire to fly them. I preferred to make them out of paper.

In 1943, as I sat down at the kitchen table for breakfast one day, my mother opened a box of Wheaties and poured the cereal into my bowl. Then the milk from a glass milk bottle followed. She put the box down on the table right in front of me and walked away. Spooning down the flakes, I reached out for the box to see what was on the back side.

WOW! It was a U.S. Navy Grumman Hellcat fighter plane that I could cut out and assemble. I couldn't wait. Pouring the entire box of Wheaties into a big mixing bowl, I got to work immediately. The instructions called for Scotch-taping a penny to the front end of the fuselage to give it forward weight. That I did. And then I took the plane outside and threw it. *Boy, did that baby fly!* It was only when I returned to the kitchen and saw my mother examining the big bowl of flakes and the scraps of the box I had left all over the table that I realized I would be eating Wheaties for many mornings to come.

Later, I discovered balsawood gliders and spent hours assembling them and throwing them up into the air. Then something compelled me to start drawing airplanes. Maybe it was the comic strip called "Smilin' Jack" that inspired me. I could count on seeing a plane nicely drawn in at least one panel every week in the *New York Sunday News.* Airplanes roared around the margins of all my school note-books. But they usually weren't real planes. I was definitely not in-terested in making accurate, lifelike representations. My planes had motors and wings and fuselages and tails the way I *thought* they should look. It didn't occur to me that they would probably never get off the ground. I was not an engineer. I was an artist.

The *Hindenburg*,
awesome in flight as well
as in its last moments on
earth, literally exploded
man's dreams of using
airships for human
transportation.
(The Bettmann Archive)

CHAPTER TWO

Caught Up in Flight

In May 1937, back in Reading, Pennsylvania, Floyd Fogleman was playing out in the yard when a car pulled up in front of his house. It was his uncle, who had come on one of his weekend visits. Uncle Joe was a veterinarian in the Washington, D.C., area, and accompanying him up the walk leading to the house was a four-legged creature that looked extremely ferocious. Floyd found himself face to face with a mean-looking German bulldog that he would get to know better over several weekends to come. He would discover that this dog with the frightening face possessed the heart and temperament of a pussycat. And he would also learn that the dog had survived a harrowing experience. The mascot of the ill-fated Hindenburg, it had been aboard on the dirigible's last flight from Friedrichshafen, Germany. Miraculously, the dog had escaped unharmed when the giant airship exploded in a ball of flame. It was now being cared for by Uncle Joe until arrangements could be made to return it to its homeland._

Floyd and his family lived near the Reading airport, so it was natural for him to go over and watch the planes that took off and landed or were lined up in a row along the edge of a taxi runway. He, too, was fascinated by airplanes, but from the very first, perhaps with Uncle Joe's bulldog in mind, he was less concerned with how they looked than with how they flew.

He soon began building simple stick-and-tissue-paper models, which were launched into flight—and to almost certain destruction—by the power of a wound-up rubber band. Then came larger and more complicated gas-powered, "free-flight" models. He would take these to an open field, set their rudders at a slight angle so they would fly in a wide circle, and then pray they would be recovered in one piece when the flight was over. But the free-flight models had too high a mortality rate for Floyd. He preferred the U-control models that were flown at the ends of wire controls. By the time radio-controlled models were introduced, it was too late for Floyd. He was flying the real thing.

His first flight occurred when he least expected it at an airport with a sign offering an airplane ride to those who felt daring. Much to his surprise, Floyd was able to talk his parents into letting him climb into the rear cockpit of a Fairchild PT-19, and soon he was waving good-bye as the plane taxied into position for takeoff. Then the plane sped down the runway and lifted off the ground, and Floyd experienced that indescribable rush of excitement that every first-time flier knows so well, that elation and exhilaration as you break free from the ground and float effortlessly upward into the heavens.

He was flying. He was soaring. But suddenly he was jolted back to reality by the pilot banging on the side of the fuselage. Floyd realized that the pilot was trying to tell him something. "You want me to what? Take the stick? OKAY!" exclaimed Floyd over the roar of the engine. At that moment he experienced an entirely different sensation. Flying an airplane at the age of sixteen, he had conquered the earth and the sky. He was in control. That was it: He knew he wanted more of this. He had to learn to fly.

He would not realize his dream until many years later. Meanwhile he became a photographic retoucher, and the careful workmanship and the long hours of concentration that had enabled him to build many model aircraft guaranteed success in his profession. When a photograph is taken for commercial purposes, it is almost never reproduced exactly as it originally appears. It may contain minor flaws that must be corrected. Or it may even require major reconstruction, including stripping several photographs together and making them appear to be a single picture. Floyd's early interest in what made an airplane fly found expression in the intricate combination of art and skill that ensures a perfect photograph.

Floyd married and moved to New Jersey. His business flourished, and at last the time was right to fulfill that long-buried dream: it was time to learn to fly. His first solo flight was out of Teterboro Airport in Teterboro, New Jersey, in a plane that was considered to be the classic training plane of its day—a Piper Cub. He soon qualified as a student pilot and was ready to undertake his first cross-country solo flight for the books.

This required flying some distance from the home airport, making sure to log in at two stops along the way. The course Floyd selected to fly was from Morristown to Boston and back. First checking on the weather, which was good, he bade good-bye to Morristown on the day of his flight. Everything went smoothly until he was approaching Springfield, Massachusetts. The weather began to look bad. But that was not the only problem. Floyd suddenly realized he had to go to the bathroom, and his plane, a Cessna 172 single-engine, high-wing monoplane, did not offer the necessary facilities. Quickly, he located a small airport behind his present position, which meant he would have to backtrack, but nature was calling and would not be denied. He made his landing in northern Connecticut, and before the propeller had finished turning he was in flight to the nearest bathroom. The romance and exhilaration of flying aside, Floyd had an eye for practical solutions to its more mundane problems.

He completed his cross-country flight and later qualified in a Piper Tri-Pacer and a Cessna 150, 172, and 182. But then his wife Margaret urged him to consider becoming pilot of a boat. That form of travel was less harrowing and he could spend more time with his growing family. How could he argue with such logic? So he traded his propeller for a rudder and found himself at the helm of a thirty-one-foot Sports Fisherman, and later a thirty-six-foot Trojan Tri-Cabin. He had drifted away from his love of flying, but his interest would later be revived in a way he could never have imagined.

As kids, both Floyd and I eagerly followed the adventures of Zack Mosely's "Smilin' Jack." They inspired me to start drawing airplanes, which led to my career in art. They inspired Floyd to build model planes, and then, later, to fly the real thing.

CHAPTER THREE

Flight into Fantasy

Early in 1955 I found myself headed for New York City to enroll at the School of Visual Arts to study illustration and graphic design. My interest in drawing airplanes had faded when I found that I much preferred drawing girls. But in order to make a living I decided upon a career in commercial art, and upon completion of a three-year course I gravitated toward the advertising business. Eventually I became an art director at a very big and very busy agency, a creative but demanding job. And one day in 1965, sitting at my desk waiting for an inspiration to come for my current assignment, I absentmindedly folded a paper airplane. It was the standard model that we all made as kids: a fold down the middle, two more triangular folds for the nose, lengthwise folds for the wings. I threw it into the air and watched it plunge ignominiously to the floor not more than two feet from my desk.

"I can do better than that."

The challenge came from the copywriter who was working with me on this assignment. And a competition was born.

In the following weeks, our paper planes became much more sophisticated and our contests keen. I won the flight for distance down the long hallway outside my office. He was the first to perfect a model that would loop over the fluorescent lights suspended from the ceiling. Our coworkers regarded our activities with some amusement. But we were "creative types," allowed certain small eccentricities. Still, I was not in the business of manufacturing paper airplanes. So I began experimenting with new models at home, folding them on the kitchen table to the puzzlement of my wife and the delight of my young son. Those that worked I carried carefully in my briefcase back to the office for the next round in the competition with the writer.

The building we worked in was located on 42nd Street, just across from the New York Public Library. My office, a lofty twenty-four floors above the street, faced south, overlooking midtown Manhattan with Bryant Park to the right. And my window, devised for the dual purpose of admitting light *and* fresh air, actually opened. One spring morning the writer opened it as I was sitting at my drawing table, engrossed in solving a graphic problem. Then he said with a devilish grin, "Dick, look. Isn't that your plane flying out there?"

I looked up in disbelief. There was indeed a paper plane hovering outside my window, and when I turned to the spot on the drawing table where my plane had been sitting, it was gone. *He had thrown my favorite paper plane out the window!*

His motive was quite clear to me. I had designed a model he could not beat, and he had launched it on a flight from which it would never return. I watched helplessly as it floated away and gradually descended to the street. But then I realized that he had merely opened up a new event in our competition—and a new horizon for me. The sight of my plane moving gracefully through the air on a bold adventure into the unknown was an experience I wanted to repeat over and over again. I was hooked. Many planes of many different designs followed that first one out the window as I searched for the one design that would give me the longest, most sustained flight.

In 1966, *Scientific American* ran a full-page ad in *The New York Times* to attract new readership to the magazine. It announced the First International Paper Airplane Competition and asked for entries from anyone who fancied himself a paper-plane enthusiast. To stimulate dreams of glory, the copy in the ad noted the similarity between classical paper airplanes and the designs that had been presented by Lockheed Aircraft and Boeing in a competition to build America's first supersonic transport. The British and French had already beaten us to the punch and were combining forces to build an SST that would be christened the Concorde. *Scientific American* wanted to know if there was someone out there at that very moment flying a paper plane down a hallway or off a balcony who might have produced a design that would make the SST thirty years obsolete.

I accepted the challenge and decided to submit one of my models. It was similar to #7, the Gypsy Moth, illustrated in the last part of this book, and I entered it in the Aerobatic/Nonprofessional class. I did not want to submit what I considered my best model, however, because I hoped to produce it as a toy at some later date.

Sadly, my entry disappeared along with thousands of others in a sea of multicolored pulp. But there was one consolation. When *The*

A model similar to the one I submitted to the First International Paper Airplane Competition.

Great International Paper Airplane Book appeared in 1967, a picture on page 17 showed Gerard Piel, publisher of *Scientific American*, sitting at his desk holding a paper plane. And there, in the lower right foreground of the photograph, was my Gypsy Moth. I recognized the blunt leading edge of the wing, the open tail section with the opened flaps, and the way I made all my fuselages. Surely that was the plane I had entered. I had delivered it personally to Mr. Piel since his office was only a few blocks away. I might just as well have thrown it out my window.

So much for becoming an aeronautical pioneer. But on further study, I found that none of the other planes shown in the book resembled my model. If it was so unique in design, perhaps it was time to approach some toy company. I wrote letters to Kenner, Mattel, Ideal, Remco, and several others, but they showed no interest in my design. I was at a dead end.

I continued to experiment with many different designs, but none seemed to fly in the way I envisioned. I wanted to make a paper plane that I could throw and that would climb high into the air, then level off by itself and go into a long, graceful glide. Our kitchen table became a paper-airplane factory. I tried first one thing, then another, until slowly I began to evolve a model that was very stable in flight. Playing around with the folds of paper on one model, I decided to open a narrow pocket on the underside of each wing. And when I did that, I noticed that the plane seemed to have even greater stability.

Next, I looked at the fuselage. If the plane struck a wall or other hard surface, the nose would bend out of shape and affect the next flight, so I folded the tip of the nose up and back into the fuselage.

Then I taped the fuselage and wings tightly together at the nose but allowed the fuselage to separate into a V shape running back to the tail section. Finally I decided to glue the separated sections together with rubber cement. Now the plane was a single, continuous surface that had very good structural integrity and would remain firmly bound together when thrown with force or buffeted by strong winds. From a flat piece of paper I had folded a configuration that I thought would fly well. But would it make that elusive flight that I had imagined so many times before?

I made a number of these newly designed models and went out to a nearby ball field to test them. I threw them into the air, one after another, but something went wrong with every flight. Inside they had worked beautifully, but outside it was a different story. They all went off line as soon as they left my hand, either to the left or to the right, nosing into the ground. I was extremely disappointed. Then I examined one of the planes, looking at it head-on, and I noticed that one wing pocket appeared larger than the opposite wing pocket. After a few more test flights, I observed that the plane always nosed over on the side that had the larger pocket. Perhaps that was causing the problem.

Carefully refolding both wings and making them look as symmetrical as possible, I again threw the plane into the air. It went out straight from my hand, climbed about as high as a telephone pole, leveled off as if it were being flown by an invisible pilot, and then proceeded to go into a long, graceful glide. *The flight was exactly as I had pictured it in my imagination!*

I launched the plane once more, and once more it soared and landed some distance away in a perfect flight. Was it a fluke, I wondered? I refolded a second model exactly like the first and threw it. *Another perfect flight.* I was able to make the same maneuver happen over and over again. That ball field had become my Kitty Hawk.

The plane factory on the kitchen table now went into full production. My son and I spent many a Saturday or Sunday afternoon test-flying paper planes from schoolyards and other fields and from the rooftop of our apartment building. But the supreme test was the flight from my office window.

I still have fond memories of some of the outstanding flights I had from that ideal launching pad. Once when I threw a plane out the window into a rather strong crosswind, it made a very sharp turn to the left and disappeared. It was a disappointing flight indeed in view of all the care and attention that had gone into building that plane. But the art director who had an office four doors down the hall came walking into my office several minutes later and said, "Are you looking for this?" It seemed that after my plane had hung a sharp left, it had glided through his open window and had made a perfect landing in the middle of his drawing table.

Another time, I sent a plane out the window and it headed in the direction of the New York Public Library. It was a very calm, slightly overcast day with a mild breeze blowing from the northwest. As the plane circled over the library, it lost altitude and slowly began its approach to the inner courtyard of the building. Lower and lower it went until it was well inside the courtyard and was finally out of sight. I had experienced my first and only hole in one.

I was also able to record my first and only landing in Bryant Park. Because of the strong wind currents, my planes were usually carried either west or east, but on this particular day the wind was just right. The plane crossed the street, cleared a row of trees, and put down gently right in the middle of the park.

Another time, there was a light mist in the air when I launched a plane. It first headed west over 42nd Street, maintaining its altitude, then turned around slowly and headed due east. But suddenly, as if struck by antiaircraft fire from below, it went into a wild tailspin completely out of control. The moisture in the air had warped the configuration of the wings, and the flight was unceremoniously terminated on the pavement of the street.

I also made night flights whenever I worked late. From my office window, the Empire State Building looked like a giant control tower off in the distance, its searchlights piercing the sky for many miles. As I launched my planes into the darkness, I used to imagine that they were real planes on real flights, guided to safe landings by the lights on top of that proud old building. They were, of course, visible only for a few moments and, far from landing safely, were probably crushed by the wheels of taxis or trod indifferently under pedestrians' feet. What did it matter that I had created the Ultimate Paper Airplane? Of what use was it to me or to anyone else? I was certainly no Leonardo, waiting for the world to catch up with me. The world had other things to think about than a man who folded pieces of paper and threw them out of his office window. But there was one consolation. I did have fun.

Over the centuries, man's unquenchable desire to conquer space has led to amazing and fanciful inventions—often with grave consequences.
(The Bettmann Archive)

CHAPTER FOUR

Fantasy Becomes Reality

In advertising, photography is often used to express an idea about a product. And retouching, as I have already mentioned, is often needed to remove the imperfections and make corrections in a photograph. Floyd Fogleman had always done a terrific job of retouching for me in the past, and one day in 1969 it was time to call on him again. When he arrived at my office, I reached into my desk drawer and pulled out one of my best planes. "Hey, Floyd, watch this," I said. I went out into the hall and threw the plane straight down the corridor. It left my hand, began to climb, then, reaching what would be a stall for normal paper planes, leveled off and continued in a gradual descent until it made a landing far down the hallway.

Floyd stood still for a moment, then raced down the hall to retrieve the plane. He came walking back very slowly, studying the underside of the plane all the way.

"What are you looking at?" I asked.

"I think you've got a whole new concept in aerodynamics here," he calmly replied.

"You're kidding me, Floyd."

"No, I'm dead serious. I've never seen anything fly quite like this. It doesn't seem to stall, and for such a short wingspan it's extremely stable. It must have something to do with the airfoil."

I gave Floyd a blank look. "What's an airfoil?"

"It's any surface like a wing or a rudder that's designed to create certain reactions as air moves around it. All the wings I've ever seen are rounded and tapered. You've folded these wings so there's a little step on the airfoil. That's new."

"How do you know so much about airfoils?" I asked suspiciously. Floyd was putting me on.

"Well, I used to make model airplanes when I was a kid," he said. "And I'm a pilot—or I used to be until I got interested in boats."

I still wasn't sure Floyd was serious, but two could play that game. "Okay," I said, "I've just revolutionized the airfoil. What should we do about it?"

Floyd thought for a moment and then proposed to take two of my paper planes home with him. The first step would be to try to duplicate the rather complex wing design in balsawood. Two days later he returned to my office with a cigar box. Inside was a balsawood glider that looked very much like my paper plane. But would it fly the same way? Floyd had a big grin on his face. He already knew the answer to that one.

I had to experience the flight of the wooden model for myself. And sure enough, I could recognize the same motion I had seen so many times before. But now what should we do?

According to Floyd, if the airfoil was indeed an entirely new concept, perhaps it was something we might be able to patent. First, though, we would need to know whether or not anything like it had ever been patented before. During more than seventy years of aviation, hundreds if not thousands of aerodynamics patents must have been issued. To me, the chances of obtaining a patent on this design seemed very slim. But Floyd was not discouraged. He knew a man who might be able to help us by conducting a patent search—Orin Severin, a retired patent attorney living in Upper Montclair, New Jersey.

Floyd told me that Severin had worked for Curtiss-Wright, a manufacturer of aircraft, during his long career. The company bore the names of aviation's greatest pioneers: Wilbur and Orville Wright, and Glenn Hammond Curtiss, whose many aeronautical achievements included the first public mile in an airplane, the *June Bug*. He had also developed the first flying boat and hydroaeroplane along with numerous other aviation advancements. Yet today the names of the Wright brothers and Glenn Curtiss, as aircraft manufacturers, have long since fallen out of the aviation business. Sadly, Curtiss-Wright made a fatal mistake when the company committed itself to building planes for commercial aviation using propjet engines, which consumed less fuel than jet engines did. Other companies turned to making planes using pure jet engines because everybody wanted to fly faster and faster and fuel economy wasn't very important then. If Curtiss-Wright had guessed wrong, what chance did Floyd and I have in the aviation business?

Finally a day was set to meet with Orin Severin. It was a Saturday in the spring of 1969, and I remember driving out to New Jersey along Route 46 to rendezvous with Floyd at one of the many shopping malls on that road. I parked my car and nervously made a few practice throws while waiting for him to show up. When he arrived, we headed for Watchung Avenue, where Mr. Severin lived.

We rang the bell and waited. The door opened and there stood a small, slender man wearing rimless spectacles who had an air of great dignity and integrity about him. He invited us in, we sat down at his dining-room table, and, as Floyd described our intentions, I handed Mr. Severin a paper plane. He looked at it carefully along with some drawings Floyd had made of the wing's cross section. And he listened very closely but hardly said a word. Then the three of us put on our jackets and went out to a ball field nearby. There I launched several planes into the sky one after the other. To my great relief, they performed beautifully. But Mr. Severin said nothing, and we returned to his house.

I was beginning to doubt that anything would come of this visit. There didn't seem to be any kind of positive reaction from Mr. Severin, but he finally said he would be willing to conduct a patent search for us and learn what prior patents we might be up against. The search would be done in the category "Airfoil for Aircraft."

Several weeks went by and I began to suspect the worst. Obviously Mr. Severin thought we were crazy and had tossed Floyd's drawings into the wastebasket as soon as we left his house. Or he had conducted the patent search, discovered there were no infringements, and had taken out a patent in his own name. He would become a multimillionaire while Floyd and I would live and die in poverty. As it happened, Mr. Severin did conduct the search and found nothing similar in the airfoil category. Incredible.

The way was now open for Floyd and me to apply for a patent. And as naive as I was, I knew that would be much more complicated than tossing a few paper planes around the U.S. Patent Office. Our education was about to begin. Mr. Severin advised us to find an aerodynamicist who would be willing to work with us and produce the mathematical formula needed to file a patent application along with the appropriate drawings, which Floyd would render.

Filing for a patent can be a very tricky business, Mr. Severin warned us. If one is too specific in defining the area one wishes to claim, others can alter the invention just enough to move in alongside with their own devices and possibly improvements as well. But if one is too broad in one's definition, then the application will be shot down by the Patent Office many times over, because the broader one's claim, the more likely one is to tread on someone else's patent rights.

Floyd and I didn't yet know what area we wished to claim, large or small. Finding an aerodynamicist was our next step, and we went to Floyd's cousin, Dick Cozzi, who worked for Pan Am. Perhaps he could help us. We paid him a visit one evening at his parents' home in Yonkers. The flight characteristics of the plane were demonstrated once again, and Dick's reactions were very positive. Yes, he did know an aerodynamicist who might be willing to help. His name: Bill Churchill.

A few days later, we all went out to visit Bill Churchill at his home in Whitestone, Queens. As we sat together at another kitchen table, he told us that he had done some work at one time on the Bousse Bi-Wing, whatever that was, and he taught at the Academy of Aeronautics in Queens, New York. We told him about our idea and showed him the drawings of the airfoil. We knew it worked, we said, but we didn't know why.

Bill was definitely interested and said he would need an airfoil cross section or planform that he could test in a wind tunnel at the school. Floyd had anticipated that request and had already constructed a planform out of balsawood. It looked like the paper plane without a fuselage or tail section. Bill examined it and said he could start with that. But four tiny eyelets would have to be drilled into the front tip, both sides of the wings, and the back in order to suspend it in the wind tunnel.

We met a few weeks later at the Academy of Aeronautics to run our first preliminary test. Dick Cozzi did not come along that evening because he had more important things on his mind: he was getting married in a few weeks. But Floyd and I had only one thing on our minds: why the airfoil worked, *if* it worked.

We entered a room at the school where Bill showed us a primitive wind tunnel powered by an old Franklin engine that was apparently in no mood to cooperate with the evening's experiment. Bill tried to start it up, but it just flatly refused. He kept tinkering with it, it kept coughing and dying. Finally, the ancient engine began to work, but Bill had to stop it so he could attach the planform in position. That accomplished, the engine cooperated by pushing air around the planform the way it was supposed to until suddenly one of the eyelets broke loose and the planform began flapping wildly. The engine was shut off again. Had the Wright brothers ever known such frustration?

After some repairs were made, the engine started without a hitch, and I watched wide-eyed as the front nose of the planform pointed slightly downward in this trial by wind. "Oh-oh," I muttered, "that's probably bad news."

"No, that's good news," Bill countered. "You see, you want an airplane to fly with a favorable nose-down attitude, because it has to fly around a circle, which is the earth. It would be very inefficient otherwise."

Bill also noted that the planform appeared very stable, but the test was not conclusive as far as learning about lift-over-drag ratios. For that, he would need an airfoil cross section at least a foot long and very uniform its full length. With that he could generate the kind of test results that could be compared to those of conventional airfoils.

Weeks later we met once again at the school, and this time we had access to a wind tunnel that was of more recent vintage. It was in Churchill's classroom, where the cross section that Floyd had made in his basement would now undergo the first real test of viability. Made out of a sheet of metal that had been carefully folded back along its length and glued to a piece of hardwood, the cross section resembled the shape of the airfoil cross section found on the paper plane.

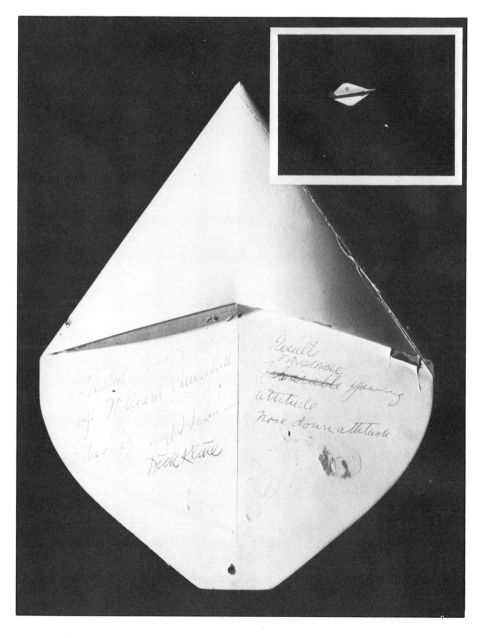

A view of the planform from the underside. It follows the wing configuration on the paper plane (inset photo) and was tested on July 8, 1969, by William Churchill at the Academy of Aeronautics. Written on the right side: Results favorable; yawing attitude, nose-down attitude.

Bill ran some quick tests, carefully jotting down the readings. Then he turned the airfoil cross section upside down. In the first tests, the step-wing configuration had been on the bottom. Now it was on top. More readings were taken and Bill observed that, whether it was tested with the step on the bottom or on the top, the airfoil did not seem to reach a stall, even up to the maximum angle, which was twenty-four degrees.

That was quite unusual, to say the least. Most conventional airfoils begin to lose their lift at about sixteen or seventeen degrees. Maybe we *did* have a whole new concept in aerodynamics. But it would be up to Churchill to work out the parameters of this strange-looking airfoil and provide Orin Severin with all the information necessary for writing up an abstract for a patent application.

We christened the invention the Kline-Fogleman airfoil, and finally, after many meetings, the papers were completed. Floyd and I flew to Washington, D.C., on March 17, 1971, to file our application in person. Located in a large building in an area called Silver City outside of Washington, the U.S. Patent Office had an air of solemnity about it. Instinctively our voices dropped to a whisper as we entered, and I became aware of the sound of my footsteps when we walked toward an open window with a serious man sitting on the other side. We handed over our claim, a signed receipt was handed to us, and after a few minutes of browsing around we left. We walked outside into the bright sunlight and started down the steps. It was finished. What had taken us more than two years to complete was now over in less than five minutes.

That night we stopped at a restaurant to celebrate and ended up wearing ridiculous green-plastic derbies in honor of St. Patrick's Day. Very undignified for two men on the threshold of aerodynamic immortality. Yet we knew that it was really just the beginning of a long struggle to overcome all the objections that the Patent Office would throw at us.

Our initial concern was whether or not the U.S. government would clamp a national-security lid on our bid to acquire a patent. If it was decided that the airfoil had military application, we would be out of luck. Six months passed and we got our answer. It was a rejection—the first of several, which we came to learn was quite normal. But at least we had gotten over the first hurdle.

There were many others, but finally in the fall of 1972 we received a call from Mr. Severin telling us that the Patent Office was officially granting us a patent. It was No. 3,706,430, the first of two patents that we were granted for a steplike discontinuity midway back on an airfoil for aircraft and for helicopter and propeller blades. Floyd and I were now among a very select company. We had an official certificate to prove it.

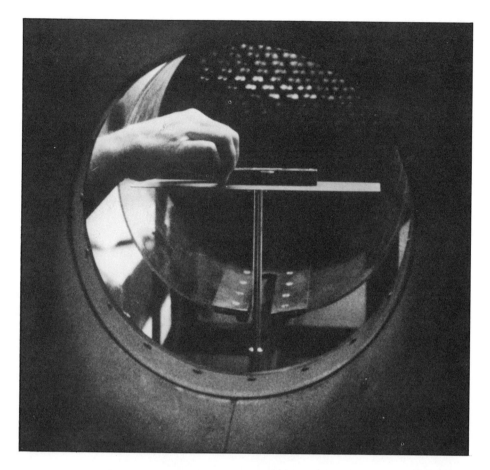

A view from the rear of the wind tunnel at the Academy of Aeronautics. The hand is that of Bill Churchill, as he checks to make sure the Kline-Fogleman airfoil is level, prior to beginning the very first wind-tunnel test.

Left to right: I, Bill Churchill, and Floyd. Behind us is the wind tunnel that was used for the tests. The picture was taken on November 11, 1970.

Official patent certificate No. 3,706,430 issued to Floyd and me.

CHAPTER FIVE

The Realities of Aerodynamics

Obtaining a patent was not the end, we soon realized. It was just the beginning. Now Floyd and I were faced with the challenge of creating some interest in our idea on the part of the aerodynamics community.

Our first break came later in 1972, through an account executive named Warren Buchanan who was working on a new product: a revolutionary golf ball designed to go at least six yards farther than a conventional golf ball. Since we were both at the same agency, we got into a conversation about the ball, and Buchanan told me that the creative team working on it had come up with the idea of getting a leading aerodynamicist to endorse it—providing it met with his approval. That man was Dr. John Nicolaides, who was professor of aerospace science and founder of the Department of Aerospace Engineering at Notre Dame University in South Bend, Indiana. He had also previously worked for the National Aeronautics and Space Administration (NASA).

As it turned out, the golf-ball idea did not fly commercially. The ball had hexagonal dimples rather than ordinary round ones and did, in fact, travel an additional six yards—but not necessarily in the direction the golfer wanted it to. The ball exaggerated the slightest mistake, and if it was hooked or sliced, it would travel even farther off line. As a result, the golfer had to make contact almost perfectly, which most golfers don't very often do, or he would find himself hitting out of the rough all day. But these problems surfaced only after the ball had been aerodynamically designed and tested successfully in a smoke tunnel. Nobody knew how it would perform until it was actually used on a golf course. There, figuratively speaking, the golf ball ended up six feet under instead of traveling six yards farther.

I asked Buchanan, who was heading out to see Dr. Nicolaides on the golf-ball project, if he would be willing to drop off a paper plane with the doctor and get his reaction. He said yes, and the paper plane took off for South Bend, Indiana, on its first flight as a passenger. Days later, the answer came back from Nicolaides: he was interested and wanted to know when Floyd and I could come out to see him.

We wasted no time. I filled a portable metal file container with paper planes, Floyd packed the metal cross section of the wing that he had made for the early wind-tunnel tests at the Academy of Aeronautics, and we took off for South Bend.

At Notre Dame, we met Dr. Nicolaides in his aerospace sciences laboratory, where various experiments were conducted and where I got my first look at that new golf ball I had heard so much about. But there was more to see, and Dr. Nicolaides showed us his pet project. He had designed a go-cart-type airplane with a Volkswagen engine. For a lifting device it used a "parawing," which filled up with air when pushed out of a high-flying cargo plane. The "parawing" would open like a horizontal parachute and form itself into the shape of an airfoil. Dr. Nicolaides would later appear on CBS's "60 Minutes" with his invention and in *Omni* magazine.

The aerospace laboratory, however, was not adequate for demonstrating the flight of the paper plane. For that I needed a lot more room, preferably a large indoor area so Dr. Nicolaides could study the plane's glide ratio. He suggested the university's Athletic and Convocation Center, where there was a basketball court. It was just a short distance from the lab, and we soon found ourselves standing in the middle of the court in the empty arena.

"Is this big enough?" Dr. Nicolaides asked.

"Well, no, I don't think so. The ceiling's not high enough and the planes will end up in the seats," I replied. "But let's give it a try."

I took out several planes from the metal box and threw the first one as hard as I could. It flew up into the lights and disappeared from view, then shot back down and proceeded to glide off the court and up into the seats. Dr. Nicolaides was amazed.

After several more flights, we returned to the laboratory, where Floyd's cross section was set up in the smoke tunnel. A smoke tunnel sends streams of smoke over and under an object placed in the proper position. All the lights in the room are then turned off, and by pushing a button you can set off strobe lights that allow you to catch a series of glimpses of the smoke flowing above and below the object. Thus you can study the air currents and see where the drag or air turbulence develops on the surface of the object as the air moves around it. The smoke-tunnel test on the Kline-Fogleman airfoil intrigued Dr. Nicolaides, and he agreed to run a series of wind-tunnel tests to see what would turn up.

Back in New York, I moved on to another advertising agency on Manhattan's Fifth Avenue, and one day I had a casual conversation about the airfoil with Fred Lamparter, an account executive at the agency. Fred was a pilot and had flown aircraft in Vietnam. He had a half-sister who worked at *Life* magazine before it died the first time, and he thought she might be interested in hearing about a paper airplane that had inspired a patent. I met with her for lunch one day at a Chinese restaurant called Pearl's in midtown Manhattan. She listened to my story but felt that it was not right for the magazine. She suggested, however, that I call a friend of hers at *Time* magazine: Audrey Ball. This I did. We met for lunch and Audrey Ball was fascinated by my story. Then things really began to happen. She wrote the first article about the paper plane, entitled "The Paper-Plane Caper," which appeared in the April 2, 1973 issue. Then a month later, a picture of me holding one of my planes was shown on the magazine's editorial page, accompanied by a paragraph that described the many inquiries I had received in response to the article. Among them was an inquiry from the White House staff. I wondered if it could have been initiated by President Nixon, but I never found out.

The article in *Time* also piqued the interest of someone at the CBS television network and a "60 Minutes" segment was born. The

Time magazine showed these two views of the paper plane. The numbers that appear on the side of the fuselage refer to the date that I made the plane: October 19, 1972.
(Photo by Bill Pierce.)

network contacted me, and one day in May 1973 a television crew arrived in my home in Mount Vernon, New York, to begin filming the story. Morley Safer was handling the segment, and we sat at the dining-room table while I recounted the story of how it all got started and showed Safer how to make one of the planes. Safer threw his completed model and, sure enough, it flew.

"Well, I'll be damned!" he exclaimed.

To get some good shots of the plane in flight, Bill Wagner, the cameraman, needed more room. So off we went to a football field in Scarsdale, New York, where planes were sent aloft one after another. Wagner used a high-speed camera, clicking away at about 180 frames a second, which would enable the plane's flight to be shown in slow motion. When the film was later edited and aired, Frank Sinatra would be heard singing "Come Fly with Me" over that portion.

The next day, we filmed some sequences at the agency where I worked, then proceeded to the top of the sixty-five-story RCA building, where the camera crew recorded some beautiful shots of the plane flying high over New York skyscrapers with the Hudson River visible in the background. In some of the shots the plane seemed to be standing still, just floating in the air on a light breeze.

Another sequence featured Dr. Nicolaides talking about the plane—and the two amateurs who had thought of the idea. "There are outstanding ideas today that are being pooh-poohed," he said. "Then, luckily maybe one like this will come along that gets a little attention and the establishment then does give it a fair and square

Cameraman Bill Wagner fires away as I launch a flight that passes directly in front of Floyd's face. To his left is Morley Safer. To his right, producer Igor Organesoff. (Photo by Bob Rubic.)

shake. Look, after all, the Wright brothers, they weren't part of the establishment. They were just old bicycle mechanics. They were the ones who first flew, not the doctors and professors, Army and Navy and so forth. No, it was the bicycle mechanics that did it. If you look through history, you'll find very often that the theoreticians and scientists were always trying to catch up with the bicycle mechanics. Because that's where the ideas come from. And wouldn't it be great coming from a paper plane?"

CBS titled the fifteen-minute segment "How to Build a Better Mousetrap," and it was aired on "60 Minutes" the same night they showed an interview about Watergate with John Ehrlichman.

Floyd and I tried not to let comparisons to the Wright brothers go to our heads, but the amount of mail generated by the program was incredible. Scores of letters arrived daily during the first few weeks following the broadcast, and others continued to arrive many months later. Viewer response, it turned out, was one of the highest that CBS had ever experienced. The network forwarded the letters to me, and I was determined to answer as many as I could. They came from every state in the Union and from other countries, including Mexico, Canada, England, New Zealand, and Spain. The most unexpected report about the program came from an art director friend who told me that while he was in the Amazon jungles shooting a commercial, he heard someone living in that remote spot talk about the famous paper plane.

The program also proved to be one of "60 Minutes"' most popular segments, so three years later CBS aired it again. And again letters and phone calls poured in, many of them asking how CBS could show the story and not show how to make the paper plane. So Floyd and I were brought back the following week to fold a plane at the tail end of another show.

Soon after the article appeared in *Time*, the Paris *L'Express* and the daily *Times* of London picked up the story. And following the first CBS show, Floyd and I made an appearance on "Wonderama," and the "60 Minutes" film sequence of the paper plane flying over the skyscrapers of New York was shown on "Captain Kangaroo."

We were then invited to appear on the "Mike Douglas Show," which meant a trip to Philadelphia. It would be our first appearance in front of a live audience and needless to say Floyd and I were a bit nervous. While waiting for our call in the Green Room, we took turns presenting our faces to a makeup person and watched the other guests as they got ready for the show. Ken Norton, the boxer, was there with a beautiful girl on each arm, a gold ring the size of a walnut on his right hand, and numerous gold chains around his neck. With all that glitter to go along with his imposing size, he would be a hard act to follow. Then there was Henny Youngman, who made a big fuss backstage and refused to go on unless he was paid immediately. He wanted his check right then or he would take a walk. But he did go on, paid in full.

Finally, there was David Janssen, who had appeared for many years on television as "The Fugitive." Floyd and I struck up a conversation with him in the Green Room, and he turned out to be very interested in our airfoil. Floyd had made a radio-controlled model of the plane that we had with us and we showed him our wing design. Janssen was a pilot himself and flew his own airplane, a Cessna Cherokee.

At last it was our turn to go on. Mike Douglas welcomed us and we told our story to the audience. I had brought along plastic replicas that were modeled after the paper plane and were being produced as a toy by the Milton Bradley Company under the name "Sky Ace." Floyd displayed his radio-controlled aircraft to the camera, and I flew the plastic planes into the audience. Then it was time to head back home.

Milton Bradley had contacted Floyd and me after seeing the "60 Minutes" segment. We demonstrated the paper plane for them as well as the wooden models Floyd had built. They liked the way the planes flew, and after several meetings all parties signed a licensing agreement that gave Milton Bradley exclusive rights to manufacture a plastic toy glider using the Kline-Fogleman step airfoil. They christened it the "Sky Ace" and that was the model I demonstrated on the "Mike Douglas Show." But personally I wasn't pleased with the way the plane was produced because it needed frequent adjustments. Ironically, Do-Well Industries of Taiwan pirated the design, and their version flew extremely well. But since it represented an infringement on our patent rights, a cease-and-desist order was obtained by Milton Bradley's lawyers and, as far as we knew, production of the pirated version ceased. We received royalties for about three years from Milton Bradley, money that helped offset the cost of additional patent work and the expense of radio-control equipment and balsawood kits of aircraft that we used as guinea pigs in later experiments. But like the sudden burst of publicity after the "60 Minutes" segment, the money eventually stopped when the plane became too expensive for Milton Bradley to continue manufacturing.

Floyd and I enjoyed being celebrities—if only briefly. But it was also our hope that the Kline-Fogleman airfoil might have some commercial application. And we dreamed bigger dreams than of plastic toys. Remembering Do-Well Industries, and thinking that someday real airplane manufacturers all over the world might want to use our idea, we decided it was time to apply for foreign patents. A U.S. patent protects an individual's or corporation's rights only in the United States, not in foreign countries. It was important to file for a patent in every country that could possibly utilize our idea. So we contacted the law firm of Bucknam and Archer, located in Garden City, Long Island. Acquiring foreign patents can be a costly undertaking, and although we were not in the strongest financial position we filed in Canada, Great Britain, and West Germany, because those countries manufacture large numbers of aircraft.

Meanwhile, the test results had come back from Dr. Nicolaides' experiments at Notre Dame, confirming the fact that the airfoil was unstallable rightside up *or* upside down, up to a forty-five-degree angle of attack. However, when the step was placed on top, it produced better lift-over-drag ratios than when it was positioned on the bottom. In experiments that I had already conducted on the paper planes, those with the step on top flew higher and farther but they also needed a reflex action, because the airfoil's natural tendency is to fly step-down. To understand a reflex action, examine an ordinary balsawood glider. Looking at a side view, you will notice that the wing lies parallel to the glider's fuselage. But the stabilizer on the tail of the plane is tilted slightly upward from front to back. That is called a reflex, and it keeps the nose of the plane up. If you removed the stabilizer and then threw the glider, it wouldn't fly.

Since the airfoil developed better lift-over-drag ratios with the step on the top, why had Floyd and I chosen to show the step on the bottom in our patent drawings? The answer to that question goes back to World War II when, somewhere in the skies over Italy, the Allies were battling the Germans. An American pilot was flying a P-47 Thunderbolt, an extremely heavy fighter plane that was actually more effective as a fighter-bomber because it was fast but not very maneuverable in a dogfight. When the pilot put his plane into a steep dive, a strange thing happened. As the plane's speed increased, it began to vibrate as it passed from the subsonic speed range into the transsonic speed range. At that moment, he was crossing an invisible

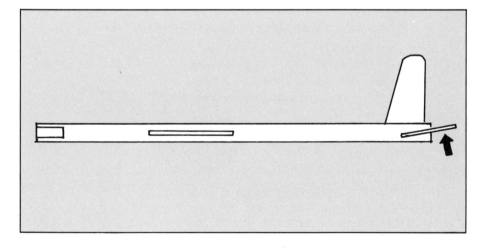

On a typical balsawood glider, the wings lie parallel to the fuselage, but the stabilizer is angled upward (see arrow). Called a reflex, it acts to keep the nose of the plane up.

barrier into the unknown. As his plane headed straight for the mountains below, he pulled back on his stick to come out of the dive. Incredibly, the plane seemed to go into an even *steeper* dive, and the mountains were rapidly approaching. Thoughts of bailing out raced through his mind, but somehow he managed to push the stick forward, perhaps to get it out of his way. The plane immediately pulled out of the dive, leaving him amazed and bewildered. An action that should have made the plane go down had, in fact, made it climb.

That pilot was one of the first to cross over into a new frontier for aircraft, which was to become known as supersonic flight. And because Floyd and I were familiar with this reverse phenomenon, we patented our airfoil with the step on the bottom rather than on the top. We foresaw possible use of the airfoil in supersonic flight, where it would pick up better lift-over-drag characteristics with the step on the bottom. The less efficient lift-over-drag ratio of this design would reverse itself in supersonic flight and become an advantage.

So far, however, with the exception of the media, nobody had paid much attention to our ideas for subsonic, supersonic, or any other kind of flight. And that, we later discovered, was also related to the patent. When we filed our original patent, the drawings showed a sharp leading edge with a step on the underside of the airfoil that started midway back, because our intention at that time was to define a *concept* that called for a step or discontinuity of surface that would allow a pocket of air to become trapped within the airfoil shape. We did *not* want to get into defining an entire airfoil configuration, simply because we did not have the knowledge, testing facilities, computers, materials, or research available to quantify the data. Our purpose was *only* to define a concept that had produced unusual results and had never been previously explored. However, others who studied our patent drawings followed them too literally.

Their test results proved to be extremely negative because the

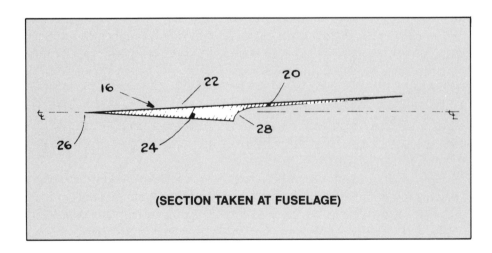

A drawing which appeared on our patent, showing the step or discontinuity on the bottom of the airfoil.

(SECTION TAKEN AT FUSELAGE)

lifting qualities of the airfoil—especially with a sharp leading edge—were very poor indeed. The entire aerodynamics community was convinced that our airfoil had no merit.

But there were two factors that had not been taken into consideration. First, although conventional airfoils are measured for the amount of vertical lift they produce, they are not tested for any *forward* pressure or push. Second, our airfoil requires a certain amount of thrust in order to trap the air turbulence created by the step, and as far as we knew only very slow-speed tests were conducted. To measure our airfoil in the same way you would measure all other designs would only produce poor results, especially if it was tested with a sharp leading edge.

But we did receive some very good test results from an unexpected source—young people who had few preconceptions and were eager to try to understand something new. First, there was Richard Foch of Titusville, Florida, who in 1974, at the age of sixteen, decided to study the Kline-Fogleman concept as a project to enter in the International Science and Engineering Fair. Richard had built a number of radio-controlled models and had noted that most planes would crash when they are flying low and had to accelerate too quickly, resulting in a stall. Then, after watching the CBS "60 Minutes" piece, he decided to try building the wing himself, to see if he could prove that our design was safer than what was presently being used. He did not have a wind tunnel at his disposal, but he was not going to let that detail stop him. He constructed a device that could be mounted on the right front fender of the family car and, with his dad driving at thirty, forty, and fifty miles per hour, he was able to take readings to learn what he needed to know in order to build his aircraft. He had, in fact, created his own wind tunnel.

On one of Richard's first test flights with his new model, the radio-controlled plane was shoved into a palm tree by an uncooperative wind, tearing off the tail and back part of the body. In disgust, he tossed the damaged plane into the air, then stood there watching in amazement as it flew even better than it had flown before. A flying wing is normally very unstable and hard to control, and Richard realized that he had come up with a flying wing that did not need a stabilizer.

His entry in the International Science and Engineering Fair, a radical, radio-controlled flying wing, won first prize, a trip to the 1974 Nobel Prize ceremonies in Sweden, and a four-year scholarship to the Florida Institute of Technology.

In 1976, fifteen-year-old Gregory Tyler from Oklahoma City, Oklahoma, designed and tested a remote-piloted supercritical airfoil using the Kline-Fogleman design. In tests against a conventional Clark "Y" airfoil, results indicated that the Kline-Fogleman airfoil was su-

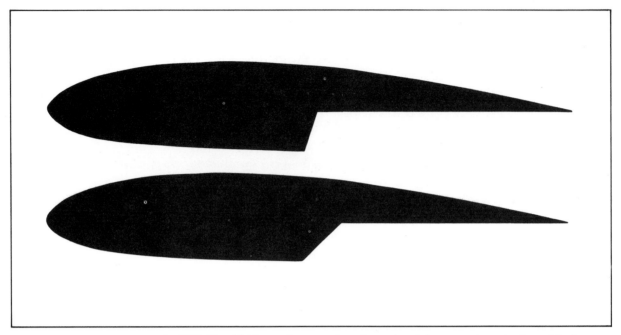

In 1980, Dan McConaughy ran a two-dimensional, low-speed smoke-tunnel test on two airfoils using the Kline-Fogleman steplike discontinuity. The 40-percent cavity (top) was tested against the 50-percent cavity (bottom). The results revealed that the 40-percent cavity trapped a pocket of air turbulence; the 50-percent cavity did not.

perior and could be utilized to improve safety and to conserve fuel in future aircraft design. Out of 450 student entries in the International Science and Engineering Fair that year, Gregory's entry landed one of the awards, plus several cash prizes.

In 1980, Dan McConaughy of Kent, Washington, did some work on the Kline-Fogleman airfoil and came up with the following conclusions: "The Kline-Fogleman wing uses separation unlike conventional airfoils." He experimented with a 40-percent cavity at the discontinuity, which had a steeper angle, and a 50-percent cavity, which had a more shallow angle. It made a difference. At a 40-percent angle it trapped a vortex in the cavity and looked exactly like the sketches I had sent him earlier, showing the flow of air inside and outside the cavity as I had visualized it. I was only imagining what was going on there, but my instincts were accurate. The 40-percent cavity worked. In contrast, the 50-percent cavity was unable to capture a pocket of air turbulence and utilize it. McConaughy concluded that using the Kline-Fogleman airfoil would make aircraft safer and, furthermore, that testing methods to date were inadequate for determining the potential of the Kline-Fogleman design.

Floyd and I were encouraged by such experiments but discouraged by the continuing lack of interest from aircraft manufacturers. We both had private doubts from time to time as to whether or not we really had something worthwhile. Yes, our airfoil would definitely make an aircraft safer. It even appeared to minimize engine torque. And because it required the center of lift and the center of gravity to be positioned closer together than normal on a radio-controlled aircraft, it also appeared to result in a better-balanced aircraft. But was it as *inefficient* as we were led to believe by so many experts? Were we just clinging to an empty dream?

Dream or not, we had continued to refine the original idea. In further experiments with the airfoil, Floyd had added flaps to the tip of the step, which allowed the aircraft to fly at a very slow speed. It also improved the landing characteristics as well as providing a means of changing direction in flight by lowering the wing flap on one side or the other. We also added a slot spoiler on the upper surface of the airfoil near the leading edge that would produce greater lift at low speed. Were these refinements worthy of another patent?

We went to the law firm of McAulay, Fields, Fisher & Goldstein, located in the Wall Street area of lower Manhattan, and with the help of Julius Fisher and Martin Goldstein we succeeded in obtaining a second patent, which incorporated several new ideas that enhanced the original design. Our second patent was granted on September 6, 1977, and numbered 4,046,338.

Floyd and I were well aware of the supercritical wing that had been developed by NASA's Dr. Richard Whitcomb during the latter part of the 1960s. This wing design was flat on top with a cambered bottom and a slight hook at the trailing edge. It seemed to hint at a cavity but did not have the sharply defined step that our design had. And the cavity was certainly not deep enough to utilize our basic concept. We would learn much later that the Whitcomb supercritical wing was turned down for a patent a number of times on the basis that it was a Clark "Y" airfoil merely turned upside down. However, in 1976 Whitcomb was finally granted a patent on his design. And with our second patent a year later, at least the U.S. Patent Office acknowledged that our design was unique.

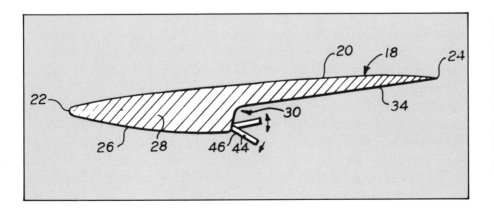

A drawing which appeared on our second patent showing flaps added to the underside at the discontinuity that would provide greater lift for slow landing speeds. The flaps could also operate independently and be used to control the aircraft by lowering one or the other in order to change direction.

But did it have any practical application? The answer to that seemed to be yes—for model airplanes. Back in 1974, through Dr. Nicolaides, Floyd and I had met with some people from Top Flite, a company in Chicago that manufactures model-airplane kits and propeller blades, and we signed a nondisclosure agreement that permitted the company to conduct experiments with our airfoil. Top Flite's chief modeler was Dan Santich, who flew radio-controlled planes in competitions around the country. He conducted the tests with a model he built called *Contender* and found that when he flew the Kline-Fogleman airfoil on a radio-controlled aircraft the lift of the wing remained constant at all speeds. Normally on a conventional airfoil, as the speed of the aircraft changes the angle of attack or pitch must be adjusted to meet the oncoming air. The consistency of lift with the Kline-Fogleman airfoil was unusual. Santich also found that the plane would not stall at very high angles of attack, another unexpected result. In fact, when he slowed the plane down to practically zero speed and it finally fell, he always had plenty of advance warning, because the plane would begin to porpoise well before the drop point in an undulating drop-glide pattern of flight.

When asked to explain how he felt the Kline-Fogleman airfoil produced its lift, Santich hypothesized that by creating a vortex within the cavity of the airfoil (the area behind the step) it produced a forward and upward push from underneath, and the vortex would therefore act as a lifting force within the shape of the airfoil. Also noting that this area seemed to expand and contract according to the speed and angle of attack, he surmised that the vortex acted as a "parasite boundary layer," which helped prevent separation or breakup of air molecules. The smooth flow of molecules over and under the airfoil is referred to as boundary-layer or laminar flow.

Santich also experimented with some of our later refinements, and when he employed a flap on the underside at the edge of the step, he found that it increased the lift during slower landing speeds. Using the Kline-Fogleman step on the tips of propeller blades, he felt that there was a noticeable increase in thrust. In short, Santich was very enthusiastic about our airfoil, but Top Flite did not wish to carry the experiments any further, and once again Floyd and I were disappointed. Today Santich is senior editor of *Model Airplane News*, a monthly magazine for model-airplane hobbyists, published in Darien, Connecticut.

Meanwhile, Floyd had been building radio-controlled models of his own, experimenting with our step configuration on both airfoils and propellers. One year he attended the RAM Show in White Plains, New York, the large East Coast trade show for radio-controlled aero modelers that is held each year at the County Center in Westchester and draws enthusiasts from all over the East. There he met Pete Reed

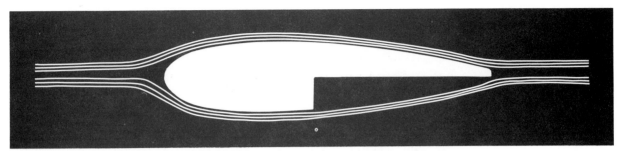

An illustration of the flow of air over and under the Kline-Fogleman airfoil as seen in a smoke-tunnel test. The pocket of compressed air becomes visible to the eye using a strobe-light effect. With this method, the "parasite boundary layer" can be clearly observed.

A radio-controlled aircraft built by Dan Santich. The Kline-Fogleman step appears on the upper surface of the wings.

Dan Santich holds the *Contender,* built with the Kline-Fogleman airfoil on the bottom surface, while Dr. Nicolaides shoots super-eight-millimeter film.

With Santich at the controls, the *Contender* makes its landing approach after a successful flight somewhere outside of Chicago.

of Avon, Connecticut, who had seen the "60 Minutes" program and was experimenting with the step on his own. Reed's interest was flying pylon racers, a type of radio-controlled model that is built for speed and competes around a very tight course. The course can be circular, diamond-shaped, or other variations, and pylon racers are very tricky to handle, especially when trying to land, because if they slow up too much on the approach they can stall and do a snap roll right into the ground. The pilot also loses all aileron control at the point when the stall occurs, so he is helpless to save the plane when it loses its lift.

After seeing several of his friends lose their planes that way,

Reed decided to put the Kline-Fogleman airfoil on the wings of his favorite pylon racer, the *Miss Dara*. He then sent her up into the sky and immediately noticed that the plane was much easier to handle. The flight was smooth and easy to control. When he brought her in for a landing, he couldn't believe it. His tiger had turned into a pussycat and was now completely docile. Reed also experimented with the step carved into a set of propeller blades and found that the prop produced more thrust and that it was easier to control the aircraft. He reported these results enthusiastically to Floyd, but chose not to enter the *Miss Dara* with the Kline-Fogleman airfoil in any of the competitions because Pylon Racing Association rules were very specific about the types of airfoils it would allow. Reed felt he would be disqualified if he entered with this unconventional wing.

So there was resistance to new ideas even in the model-airplane establishment. But there were among its members some more venturesome spirits. Floyd became friendly with Bill Wardlow, who manufactured retractable landing gears for radio-controlled aircraft and entered his planes in patternship competitions. In these competitions radio-controlled aircraft fly certain maneuvers or patterns, some of which are extremely difficult to execute. One such maneuver, the "tail-slide," calls for the pilot to take the airplane straight up as high as possible, hang it in the sky on its propeller, then back it straight down about six plane lengths, kick the stabilizer up until it levels off, then fly it straight away. This particular pattern is so difficult to do that it was banned from the competitions. But one day Wardlow flew a model that Floyd had built with our airfoil and tried this vertical maneuver, which normally fails because at the top of the plane's climb the yaw effect takes over—that is, the torque of the engine causes the plane to roll to the left, opposite the direction of the propeller, and the plane falls off line and goes into a spin. But this time was different. Six times in a row, Wardlow performed the maneuver and never once did the plane fall off line. In fact, if he wanted to put the plane into a spin he found that he had to force it, because the wing's natural tendency is to fly level with the earth at all times.

Another friend of Floyd's, Dennis Donahue of Bergenfield, New Jersey, also flew pattern ships, which are larger than pylon racers and are designed to fly over a much longer course. A pattern ship can climb to a higher altitude and execute intricate maneuvers at a much greater distance from the radio controls operated by the pilot. Donahue put one of Floyd's custom-made props on his pattern ship and sent it into the air. Then he, too, decided to try a "tail-slide." "It was real strange," he later told Floyd. The yaw effect was much less, and he felt that the increase in thrust from the Kline-Fogleman prop was between 13 and 20 percent. He could not understand why it would suddenly change the handling of his pattern ship the way it did. Others watching the maneuvers nearby were equally amazed.

Admittedly, Floyd and I were amateurs in the field of aerodynamics, but we were still puzzled by the fact that our ideas, which seemed to work very well with model aircraft, continued to meet with such indifference from the manufacturers of the real thing. But then in 1981 we were contacted by two people from Amerijet, a newly formed aircraft company in Youngstown, Ohio, to discuss a licensing agreement pertaining to our design. Amerijet wanted to produce a small business jet that would require only a single pilot instead of the two that are required by all insurance companies. Because the company felt that this new wing would make the plane much safer to operate, it would be able to get the necessary approval. The plane would also be able to land and take off from shorter runways, making it more suitable for small airports than conventional jet planes. Parties from both sides signed a licensing agreement in July 1981, and it was hoped at that time that a plane would be ready to fly in about seven years. Both Floyd and I realized that our dream of seeing a plane with our wing design in the air was now a possibility, although still a long way off.

CHAPTER SIX

Catching a Second Wind

Even before we entered into the agreement with Amerijet, someone else was also showing an interest in our paper plane. Scot Morris, a writer for *Omni* magazine, had contacted me originally in 1979 about doing an article on our airfoil that would also reveal the folding instructions for the first time. However, management at the magazine was not thrilled with the added expense such a project would incur, since it would mean devoting a center spread solely to making a pair of paper planes. It would also call for the use of a heavier grade of paper—the same weight, in fact, as the cover stock. Negotiations were off and on over a four-year period, until finally, in 1984, Morris was able to convince his people that the time was right to run the article. *Omni* wanted to come out with a special spring issue that would be backed by a heavy advertising campaign. What they needed was a big idea, and Morris felt he had it. Much of the writing and interviewing had already taken place, and he had come upon an interesting angle that he wanted to pursue. If, in fact, the Kline-Fogleman airfoil was a revolutionary new concept in aerodynamics, why wasn't it being utilized? Was there a cover-up going on, or was it a case of neglect? He was determined to find out.

The article, which appeared in the April 1984 issue of *Omni*, was illustrated by a trick shot of Floyd and me zooming through the sky with some of our paper planes and recounted the story of the airfoil from its beginnings. Dr. Nicolaides' early test results were again cited, and Floyd commented on the results of his more recent tests with radio-controlled model planes. "I tested the design with different curvatures on the top and bottom of the wing," he said, "and the most impressive thing about them all is that they don't want to spin." And he added, "Our plane just refuses to tip stall."

All that Floyd and I already knew. And we knew that NASA had tested the airfoil but, as Floyd remarked, "We couldn't get any results from them, and neither could Nicolaides." Morris got the results. Preparing for the *Omni* article back in 1979, he had interviewed P. K. Pierpont, then manager of the airfoil research program at NASA's Langley Research Center in Virginia. Pierpont knew of three studies looking into the characteristics of the Kline-Fogleman airfoil, one of which was partially funded by NASA. All three had come to the same conclusion: the Kline-Fogleman airfoil was poor as far as lift-over-drag ratios were concerned. The studies concluded that the airfoil had no practical application and no further testing was called for due to these poor results. It was dismissed as being no better than a flat plate, according to Pierpont.

Morris persisted but continued to come up against unfavorable reports. He talked to Bud Bobbitt, chief of NASA's transsonic-aerodynamics division. Bobbitt had produced similar lift-over-drag ratios and felt that the stall-resistance factor was a low priority. Max David, of the Air Force Flight Dynamics Lab at Wright-Patterson Air Force Base in Dayton, Ohio, had also found that the wing had too much drag and not enough lift.

"All that is true," Dr. Nicolaides is quoted as saying in the article, "but it misses the point. This airfoil doesn't have great lift at low angles, I grant that. But at high angles, where most planes spin out of control and crash, this one keeps flying."

Morris speculates that the government never tested the airfoil properly, or if it did it was already committed to the Whitcomb supercritical wing and may have downplayed the airworthiness of the Kline-Fogleman design. "I don't know whether the whole story will ever come out," Dr. Nicolaides is quoted as saying. "But the important thing to remember is that the Kline-Fogleman wing doesn't stall. If the government testers say that it is not quite as good as other wings in terms of lift-to-drag ratios, they are neglecting to say that it is infinitely better in terms of not killing people. That's what the Kline-Fogleman wing is all about."

Floyd and I were enormously gratified by the article, and by a favorable report from J. B. Mitroo, then president of Amerijet, the company that was actually working on putting a plane in the air with the Kline-Fogleman airfoil. Mitroo told *Omni* that their preliminary tests indicated that the wing would actually improve the efficiencies of flight, bringing about a 25 to 35 percent increase in fuel savings.

Meanwhile, testing was proceeding on another front as well. On several previous occasions, Floyd had made up sets of propeller blades and given them to people he knew who flew radio-controlled aircraft. A propeller blade is actually a rotating airfoil, as is the case with helicopter blades. Using blades manufactured by Top Flite, Floyd carved the Kline-Fogleman step into their tips at both ends. For an experiment to determine how the Kline-Fogleman propeller blade would compare to the amount of thrust produced by a conventional propeller blade, he needed two wooden blades of identical weight, both of which had to be perfectly balanced prior to testing. Unbalanced blades would put stress on the engine and affect the outcome of the test.

A friend of Floyd's, George Leu of South Orange, New Jersey, was one of the recipients of an experimental set of propeller blades. Leu had many years' experience flying radio-controlled aircraft with Floyd, and he agreed to conduct the propeller-blade test. The experimental blades were eleven inches long and had a seven-degree angle of pitch; the engine used was a Webra Speed .60 cubic inch.

Leu conducted a simple static test with a radio-controlled plane anchored to the ground. A spring-loaded fish scale was used to determine the amount of pull or thrust produced by both a conventional blade and the Kline-Fogleman prop. The results were striking. The conventional blade pulled a maximum of ten pounds. But when Leu put the Kline-Fogleman prop on, he got eleven pounds of thrust, or a 10-percent increase in thrust with slightly fewer RPMs (a 200-RPM drop in a 13,500-RPM run). The test was repeated a second time, and the results remained the same.

Then Leu put the Kline-Fogleman prop on his radio-controlled plane and flew it. He noticed that it climbed vertically with much more power than with the conventional prop that he had flown before.

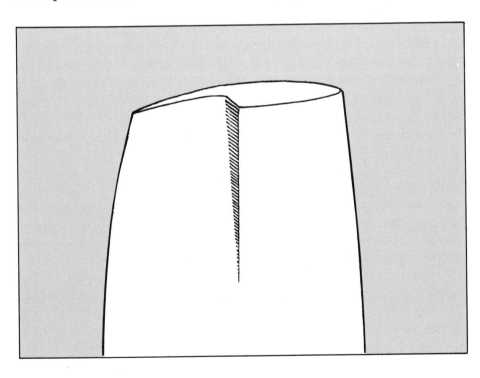

A close-up of the tip of a model-plane propeller blade with a Kline-Fogleman step carved into the tip. From leading edge to trailing edge at the tip is ¾". The length of the step measures 2".

Furthermore, the plane needed less correction than usual to do the standard maneuvers, such as rolling or looping. Leu also felt that the handling of the plane was much crisper because of the Kline-Fogleman prop. Obviously, something was happening that was rather hard to explain. The test results were passed along to Scot Morris and were included in the *Omni* article.

That issue of the magazine proved to be the largest-selling ever, and it sparked another round of media interest in our paper plane. Even before the article was published, I was asked to appear on the "David Letterman Show." On March 16, 1984, I was whisked by limousine from my home in Yonkers to the NBC studios in Manhattan's Rockefeller Center. The chauffeur was a friendly old gentleman who originally came from Hungary, and on the way into the city he talked about some of his famous passengers, among them Johnny Carson, David Letterman, Danny Thomas, and Ed McMahon. It occurred to me that *my* backside was sitting for a brief period of time in the same place where other, more famous backsides had rested. But then I remembered I had had a brief taste of fame myself ten years before—only to be quickly forgotten. It helped me keep my humility.

I was still pondering my fate as I was led from my dressing room in the studio, where I had been busily folding paper planes, down a crowded hallway, through wooden swinging doors, into a darkened corridor. And there, standing directly under a single, recessed, bright light shining down directly on top of his head, was David Letterman. "God, you're tall," I blurted.

"You've got to be in this business," Letterman shot back.

We shook hands and I was taken back to my dressing room, where I continued folding planes. Little did I know that during those few moments with Letterman I had been given the thumbs-up sign. Had he felt uneasy with me as a guest, that would have been it. I didn't know what to expect next, but finally I was summoned on stage. Letterman greeted me, we shook hands again, and I sat down at his desk. He asked me to explain what was different about our design, which I did. He made a few funny remarks, then asked me to fly some of the paper planes into the audience. I fired the first one and it sailed straight across the studio and struck the cameraman at the far edge of the stage. Letterman was impressed, and as I was driven home by the same Hungarian chauffeur I wondered if he would add my name to his list of famous passengers.

Next there was a call from *Omni* asking me to appear on the "CBS Morning News." Again a limo picked me up, this time at 6:30 A.M., and I soon found myself at the same CBS studios on West 57th Street where I had been with Floyd almost eleven years before for the "60 Minutes" segment. This time I was interviewed by Bill Kurtis and Diane Sawyer. After a discussion about the plane's characteristics, Kurtis threw two of my models, one after the other, clear across the studio, where they both struck the far wall well beyond the view of the camera.

About a month later, I made a third TV appearance on the "Regis Philbin Morning Show" on ABC. For that appearance, I brought along several silhouette diagrams that showed how our airfoil cross section looked compared to a conventional airfoil, because I had come to realize that many people assumed that our patent was for a paper airplane rather than a real one.

The *Omni* article, like the "60 Minutes" segment of a decade before, revived interest in our invention—at least among the media. But once again that interest soon faded and most of the experts remained skeptical. Floyd and I had come full circle. It seemed that we were not like the Wright Brothers after all. Their ideas had received immediate acceptance. And Wilbur and Orville never had to appear on television.

Wilbur and Orville Wright prepare for takeoff at Kitty Hawk. Their flight covered a distance of just over 122 feet in 59 seconds at an altitude of 10 feet. The greatest challenge would be to launch the Ultimate Paper Airplane from this same site and break the distance and altitude records established by the Wright brothers.
(The Bettmann Archive)

CHAPTER SEVEN

How *Do* Airplanes Fly?

There is more than one explanation for how an airplane flies, but before we talk about man-made flying machines let us first look at the marvelous creatures that first inspired man to conquer the air, the domain above the surface of the earth once belonging exclusively to birds, bats, bees, and butterflies.

A bird's wing is actually an airfoil. It produces lift, controls direction, maintains stability, and generates speed or thrust. Since strength or structural integrity combined with lightness of material is one of the key factors to achieve sustained and efficient flight, many of the bones in a bird's wing, including the long wing spars, are hollow. Marrow would only be added weight, and in the case of a bird's wing it must be sacrificed. Instead, there's a trusslike internal bracing inside the thin-walled, hollow bone that provides the necessary structural strength. Many of the bones in a bird's body are fused together as well, to provide a light but rigid airframe.

But flying takes more than a light airframe. If you have ever wondered why birds never seem to get tired from all that flapping, it is because they have a respiratory system that is like a two-cycle pump. In addition to a pair of lungs, they have two extra sets of storage sacs to hold air, called the anterior and posterior sacs. When a bird inhales, part of the fresh air passes through the lungs while the rest bypasses them and goes directly to the posterior air sacs. When the bird exhales, fresh air stored in the posterior air sacs enters the lungs while stale air in the anterior air sacs is moved directly out of the body. Thus the bird's body is supplied with a *continuous* supply of oxygen. Humans can handle only one breath of air at a time. Think what we could do if we possessed the bird's two-cycle system.

A man-made machine that flies breathes air in a different way than a bird does. It uses an engine to develop thrust, and it utilizes air in various ways according to the design of the propulsion system. For example, a jet engine uses a mixture of air and fuel to produce combustion when it is ignited. The engine has the capability to produce thrust for a certain period of time depending upon the amount of fuel the plane is able to carry.

The plane itself must contend with two sets of opposing forces when it is in flight. The first set are thrust and drag. Thrust, a positive force, pushes the airplane forward and causes it to push air out of its way. The displaced air then produces a certain amount of air turbulence or drag, which is a negative force that acts against the thrust, making the airplane less efficient. Because every protrusion on the aircraft reduces its efficiency, it is essential that the entire plane be as streamlined as possible in order to reduce the amount of drag.

Howard Hughes once had every single rivet head sanded down flush with the metal surface of his then brand-new monoplane before he flew it. He was out to set a world speed record and he realized that those thousands of bumps, tiny though they were, would resist the air and create drag. By eliminating them, he would reduce some of the drag the airplane produced and thereby increase his speed.

So the object in designing an airplane is to streamline it as much as possible to cut down on friction and therefore drag. If air could be pictured as sheets laid down one on top of another over the airplane's wing, the first sheet would stick or adhere to the upper surface of the wing as it moved through the air. The second sheet would press against the first, but it would begin to move or slide over the sheet directly below. The third and fourth sheets would move faster still. This is called *boundary-layer* or *laminar flow*. As long as the flow of air is kept smooth, the wing is performing efficiently, but if the air begins to break up, it becomes turbulent and produces resistance or drag, thus making the airplane less efficient.

Lift and gravity, or the weight of the aircraft, are the second set of opposing forces with which the airplane must contend. An airfoil serves as a lifting device and must provide sufficient lift to move the plane up into the air against the force of gravity. It must also be able to continue producing lift at various angles of attack or attitude into the wind and at various speeds. An airfoil will usually require a change in angle of attack or attitude when there is a change in air speed. This is needed in order to maximize lift efficiency.

The lifting device or airfoil that a plane uses produces its lift in at least two ways. Bernoulli's principle has been referred to most frequently as the explanation for how an airplane gets off the ground. However, many would strongly argue that Newton's law that for every action there is an equal and opposite reaction should get equal billing. As an example of that theory, a flat plate will produce some lift when it is pitched or angled upward into the oncoming air. This pitch is called the angle of attack and is crucial to maintain lift. As the flat plate pushes against the air, it deflects some air downward. This deflected air pushes against the underside of the flat plate, causing it to move upward. In other words, lift is obtained by pushing air down. If you have experienced riding in a car with your hand out the window, fingers pointed straight ahead and palm horizontal, then you know that when you turn your fingers and palm slightly upward the oncoming air pushes your hand—gives your hand a lift.

Now a conventional airfoil has a specific form or shape. It is not a flat plate. The bottom is usually flat; the front or leading edge is rounded; the top is curved or cambered in front but slopes down toward the trailing edge. The bone in a bird's wing has this camber, and the Wright brothers' first airplane imitated the same curve.

For a moment, picture yourself as a molecule of air in space with another molecule directly below you. As a conventional airfoil comes toward both of you, the molecule below you passes under the airfoil with nothing in his way. You, however, must climb up over the hill that is directly in front of you. In order to keep up with that other molecule, you must move faster over the upper surface of the wing. Because you are moving faster, the area above that part of the wing is under less pressure. Since the pressure is then greater beneath the wing, the wing is pushed upward. According to Bernoulli, the faster a gas or fluid moves, the less pressure it exerts. However, many people strongly believe that the primary lift is due to the air that the wing pushes downward—as your hand does outside the car window.

To sum up, when the wing is motionless air pressure acts *against* it on all its surfaces. There is air pressure downward on the top surface of the wing and equal air pressure upward on the bottom surface. However, when the wing is in motion, the density or pressure of the air on the surfaces of the wing is altered. The *reduction* of air pressure on the upper surface of the wing and the *increase* of air pressure on the bottom create a net upward air pressure or lift. In other words, *both* Bernoulli's principle and Newton's law cause an airplane to climb into the air.

The wing will reach a stall when it meets the air at an excessive angle of attack and is no longer able to push air downward. The low-pressure area on the upper surface may also be outweighed by air turbulence and all lift destroyed. But the wings themselves will carry an airplane just so far. The average airplane, without the guiding hand of a pilot, will not fly straight and level for very long by itself, because its tendency is to spiral dive. It will go into a wide turn, the turn will gradually tighten until it becomes a downward spiral, and finally it will go into a vicious ever-tightening nosedive. So a pilot is essential in an airplane with a conventional airfoil.

When aircraft were required to go faster and faster, conventional airfoils began to run into problems. As a wing approached the sound barrier, tremendous pressure built up on the upper surface; as the plane broke through the sound barrier, the shock waves that cause sonic boom further increased the pressure. Also, friction produced by the rush of air against the upper surface caused the skin of the aircraft to heat up. All this put a great deal of stress on the wing. A new design was needed to cope with this magnified negative force.

In 1965, Dr. Richard Whitcomb, an aeronautical engineer at NASA's Langley Research Center in Virginia, had the idea of eliminating the camber on the upper surface of the wing. He made the top surface flat and the camber emerged on the bottom or underside of the wing. This design enabled the shock waves to be pushed farther back on the upper surface, thereby reducing their devastating effects.

Two illustrations based on a NASA drawing. The top diagram shows the supersonic flow as it builds up on a conventional airfoil to a point where it produces a strong shock wave. This leads to a separation of boundary layer, as well as increased drag. The bottom diagram shows a weak shock wave, because the pressure buildup "fans out" over the flat upper surface. The cusp or hook is at the trailing edge.

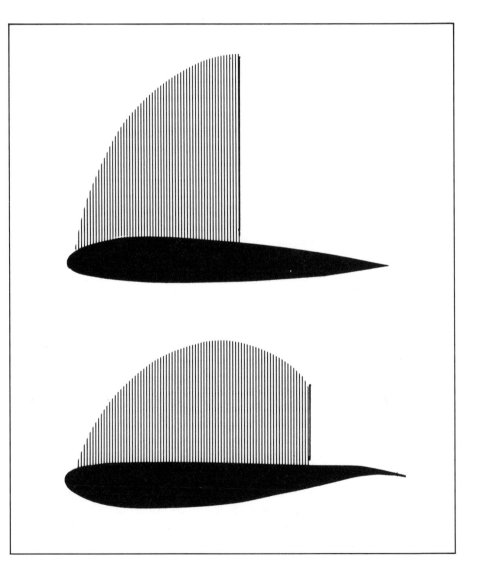

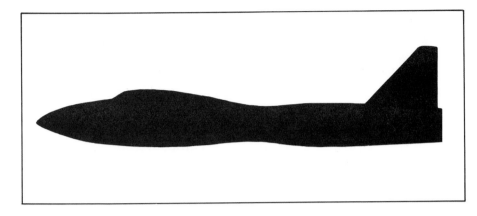

In the mid-1960s, Dr. Richard Whitcomb invented the "Coke bottle" fuselage. It has also been referred to as a "wasp waist." It made the aircraft more aerodynamically efficient at or above the speed of sound.

The drag was reduced and the airfoil became much more efficient for supersonic flight.

Whitcomb also designed a "cusp" or "hook" on the underside at the trailing edge, which helped improve efficiency as well. However, for many years, his patent application was rejected by the Patent Office. It was not until 1976, four years after we obtained our first patent for the Kline-Fogleman airfoil, that Whitcomb was granted his patent. However, the rights to that patent belong to NASA, because he developed the design as an employee.

Whitcomb was already famous for his "Coke bottle" fuselage design for supersonic aircraft (also referred to as the "wasp waist"). This design called for making a tuck or pulling in the waist of the fuselage and made it possible for an 800-mile-per-hour airplane to reach 1,000 miles per hour. The small waist or valley in the body of the fuselage enables the aircraft to move into supersonic speed with reduced sonic boom because less pressure is allowed to build up.

Normally, as a fuselage moves through air, it displaces air that then has nowhere to go. However, if there is a depression in the fuselage, some of the displaced air falls into that space and gets trapped—*it has found a home.* Thus drag is reduced and as a result there is also a smaller sonic boom.

A recent NASA natural laminar flow airfoil shows a return to the cambered upper surface with a more blunted leading edge. Because of composite material surfaces, a smoothness is achieved on the skin of the aircraft that provides a natural laminar flow up to Mach .6 (about 430 miles per hour at sea level, less at altitude), and the first layer of air adheres to the surface much better, thereby reducing friction and drag. The airfoil still retains the "cusp" or gradual cavity at the back on the underside of the trailing edge.

When I first started folding paper planes, I was ignorant of the laws and principles that enabled them to fly. I simply folded and refolded airfoil configurations until my planes worked the way I wanted them to. With his experience as a pilot and model maker,

Floyd was far more sophisticated in his understanding of flight. Even so, when we joined forces we were both exploring unknown and mysterious territory. We knew the Kline-Fogleman airfoil worked. But only after years of experimentation and investigation did we discover why.

(A) is a conventional Clark "Y" airfoil with a cambered upper surface and a flat underside.

(B) is a semisymmetrical airfoil with a slightly rounded underside.

(C) is the Whitcomb supercritical airfoil with a flat upper surface and a rounded underside.

(D) is a recent NASA natural laminar flow airfoil. It has a blunted leading edge and cambered upper surface but still retains the "cusp" on the underside at the trailing edge.

(E) is the Kline-Fogleman airfoil. Can it be the next step in the evolution of airfoils?

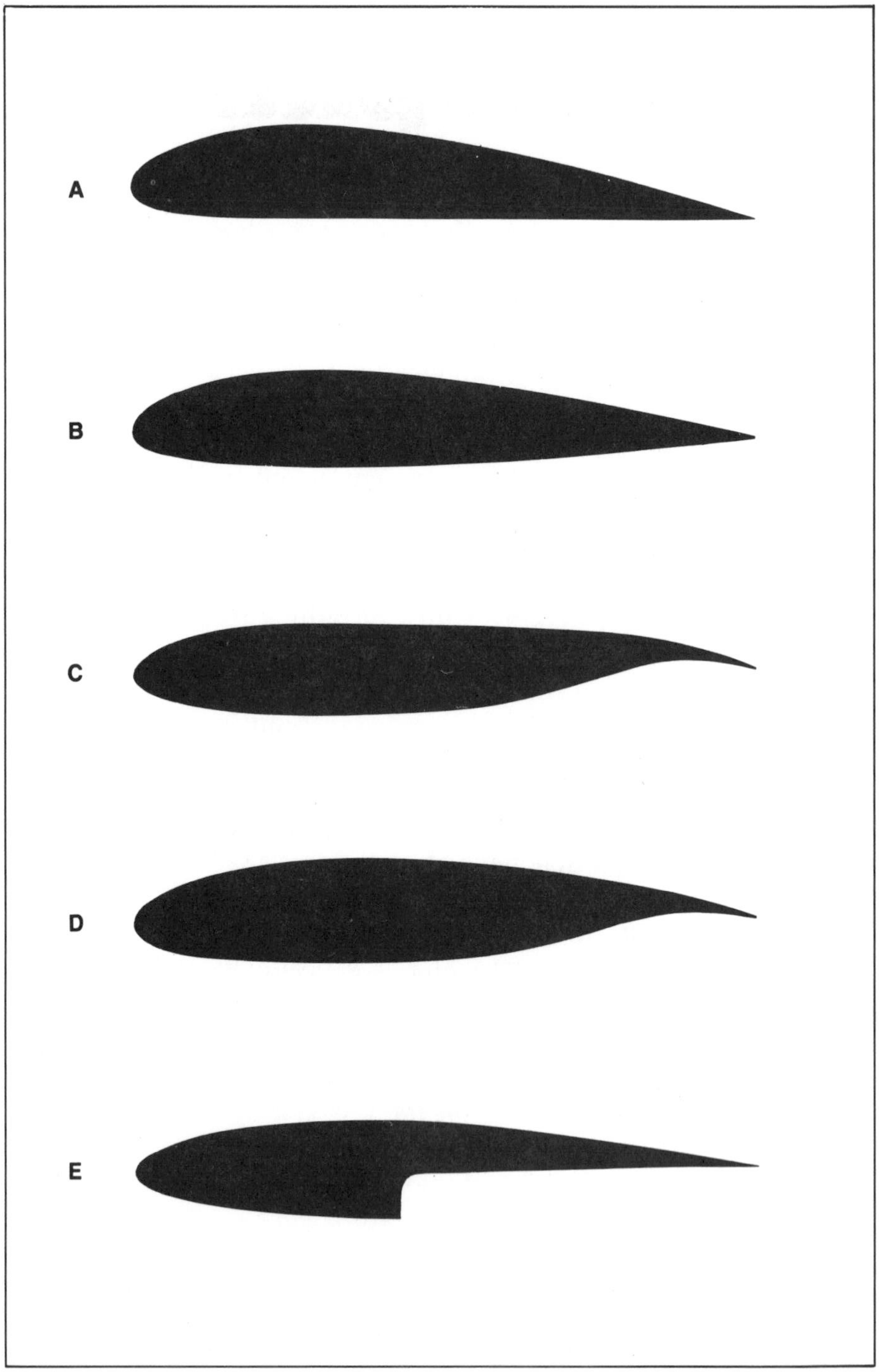

A

B

C

D

E

CHAPTER EIGHT

The Concept Explained

The Kline-Fogleman airfoil works differently from conventional airfoils. This is not to say that it operates outside of Newton's or Bernoulli's principles. But it does employ a unique method for utilizing some of the air it displaces that would otherwise cause drag. Thus it operates more efficiently than conventional airfoils.

The concept is radical because until now no one has ever thought it possible to actually utilize air turbulence to produce lift—in other words, to partially convert the negative force, drag, into the positive force, lift. The cavity created behind the steplike discontinuity of the Kline-Fogleman airfoil provides a home for some of the air turbulence. That turbulence doubles back or begins to rotate in the same direction that the airfoil is traveling, once it passes beyond the lip of the discontinuity. If you have ever watched rain water as it trickles over the edge of a roof, you may have observed that the natural tendency of the water, as it passes beyond the edge, is to change direction and move inward *behind* the lower lip of the eaves instead of continuing *forward* in the same direction. This is a result of capillary action, and since water and air share many of the same basic characteristics, it is natural to expect air to react in the same way when it passes beyond a discontinuity or step. And, in fact, it does.

The pocket of trapped, compressed air supports the aircraft at all normal angles of attack. If the aircraft's wing dips on either side, the pressure in the lower air pocket increases and forces the wing upward until it is level, thus equalizing the air pressure in both pockets once again.

While the air trapped in the airfoil's cavity exerts a forward and upward pressure, it also acts as a body filling out the rest of the airfoil configuration. This trapped-air "body" serves as a "parasite boundary

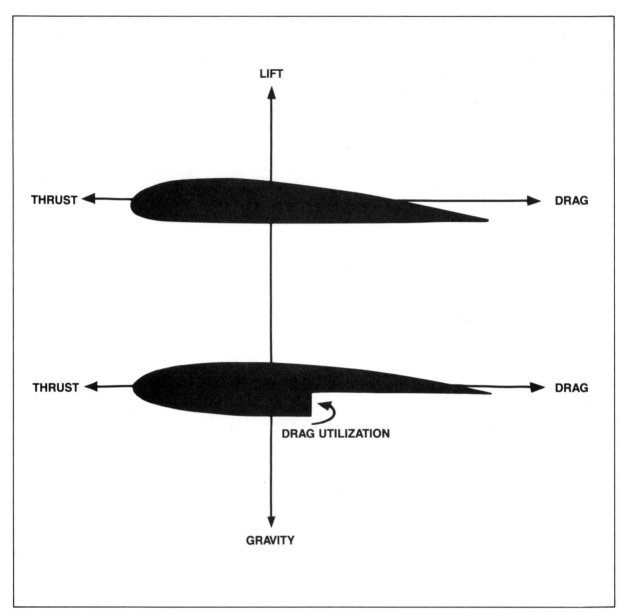

The conventional airfoil (top) shows the four major forces that act upon a wing during flight: lift, thrust, drag, and gravity. The Kline-Fogleman airfoil (bottom) traps some of the displaced air molecules, reverses their direction, and produces a forward "push." This action will support the airfoil up to a 45° angle of attack, whether it is used with the step on the bottom or on the top.

layer," enabling all other air molecules to ride past without friction. Thus drag is even further reduced.

Several unusual characteristics derive from the steplike discontinuity of the Kline-Fogleman airfoil. First, the possibility of a stall is all but eliminated. Second, horizontal stability is maintained at all times. Third, engine torque is dramatically reduced. Fourth, because the center of lift and the center of gravity must be positioned closer together than on conventional aircraft, the aircraft is better balanced. Fifth, there is much greater fuel efficiency than with a conventional airfoil or propeller blade.

Why then has the Kline-Fogleman airfoil been almost totally ignored by the people whose business it is to manufacture efficient aircraft? A full-sized aircraft has not yet been flown with the Kline-Fogleman airfoil, and it is possible that negative factors not presently known will be encountered when that is done. However, it is also possible that the Kline-Fogleman airfoil will retain the characteristics that make it so unique on a small scale. Admittedly, one drawback would be a loss of fuel capacity due to the cavity in the wing, since that is where much of an aircraft's fuel is stored. And until fairly recently it would not have been possible to construct such a wing that could withstand high stress levels because the materials and methods for its manufacture were not available. Today, however, with composite materials and honeycomb construction, that would not be a problem.

It is important to point out that the Kline-Fogleman airfoil requires a sufficient amount of thrust in order to trap and utilize a pocket of air turbulence. For subsonic flight, placing the step on top of the wing improves the lift-over-drag ratio about 44 percent. And a reflex action is also necessary. But the stall-resistant characteristic alone would probably save many lives in small aircraft. Although it is crucial for every pilot to experience a stall and learn how to overcome it, an airplane that will not stall seems highly desirable.

Another possible safety feature is the elimination of the deadly vortices that normally trail a large commercial aircraft in flight. Air turbulence spirals off the wing tips of a jumbo jet in a downward direction and can trail the aircraft for several miles and last up to two minutes. A small private plane crossing the path well behind and below the large aircraft can literally be torn apart by the turbulence. Because the Kline-Fogleman airfoil utilizes some of the air turbulence, it is possible that the severity of those dangerous vortices would be significantly reduced. However, that has yet to be proven.

The importance of aerodynamics is not limited to airplanes. Automobile makers are very interested in aerodynamic design, since it has a definite effect on the fuel efficiency of the cars they produce. The more streamlined a car is, the better gas mileage it will get because the smoother air flow reduces drag.

Recently I have observed an interesting change occurring in automotive design. There is now a step or discontinuity of surface on the rooflines of many of today's cars. While the windshield is tapered, the roofline drops off sharply at the rear window. This abrupt change in the flow of the car's line is in contrast to previous ideas of efficient design which called for a tapered line right to the end of the trunk and bumper.

When Volvo first announced its 1984 deluxe model in a series of advertisements, it claimed that the Volvo 760GLE took ten years to design, and that it was more aerodynamically efficient than a Porche 928. Coincidentally, included as part of the rear edge of its roofline design was a step.

The 1985 Chevrolet Monte Carlo also employs a step as part of its design, but with a further refinement. The trunk area directly behind the step is almost flat or horizontal instead of tapered, and at the rear edge of the trunkline there is a lip or spoiler. This rounded ridge at the rear of the trunk helps trap a bigger pocket of air and produces the "parasite boundary layer" effect. Ford's 1985 Mercury Cougar has close to a 90-degree angle on the rear edge of its roofline, but the trunkline tapers off, making it more curved. As a result, it is more difficult to trap the air pocket.

Every division of General Motors produces at least one model with a step at the rear edge of the roofline. Some of the models manufactured by Chrysler have a similar configuration, and even the Japanese are beginning to follow this trend. Is it merely a matter of style? Personally, I have never been able to obtain any information that proves our theory that a step improves aerodynamic efficiency, but I am convinced that the increasing use of the step in automotive design is not purely for aesthetic reasons.

What has been proven is that the the Kline-Fogleman concept, whether applied to a wing or to a propeller, can improve the safety of flight. Why then, if Floyd and I have indeed built a better mouse-trap, does the path to our door remain conspicuously unbeaten? Whatever the reason, when we get together every year to celebrate yet another anniversary of our first patent, Floyd and I always ponder the symbolic significance of our names. In German, Klein means "little" and Fogle or Vogel means "bird." Together, then, Kline-Fogleman might be translated as "Little Birdman." That seems appropriate enough.

CHAPTER NINE

The Ultimate Paper Airplane

With a little practice you can learn to fold and fly the Ultimate Paper Airplane. There are seven different models to choose from, each with its own unique characteristics.

Sky Hawk. This is the model that inspired the first patent. With the distinctive Kline-Fogleman step on the underside of the wing, it appeared in *Time* magazine in 1973. It was later shown on CBS's "60 Minutes," produced as a toy by the Milton Bradley Company, and published in *Omni* magazine in 1984, where the folding instructions were revealed for the first time.

Super Hawk. This model has the Kline-Fogleman step on the upper surface of the wing as well as a reflex action in the tail section. The step on top of the wing produces excellent lift. The Super Hawk should easily climb as high as a telephone pole.

Voyager. This model also has the Kline-Fogleman step on the upper surface of the wing. In addition, it has a V-shaped tail section with flaps on the fuselage, inside the tail section, that act as a reflex action. It travels a long way.

Condor. This model has a small pair of wings on the upper surface of the fuselage that act as a reflex action. Its flight performance is quite possibly the best of all the models, but that's for you to decide.

Gyrfalcon. This model also has the Kline-Fogleman step on top of the wing. It has landing gears extending from the underside of the fuselage and a high tail section. The tail section will vibrate if the plane is thrown too hard; the Gyrfalcon requires a gentle throw and a smooth runway.

Sting Ray. This model has the Kline-Fogleman step on the underside of the wing. It has a V-shaped tail section, but it does not require a reflex action.

Gypsy Moth. First made in the early 1960s, this was the prototype of the Ultimate Paper Airplane. It comes with the Kline-Fogleman step on the underside of the wing. It is excellent for making loops.

The instructions for folding and flying each of these models appear on pages 70–83. You will also find two printed patterns for each model on pages 99–126. The folds and cuts are ruled and numbered on both sides of each pattern to correspond to the step-by-step instructions. The instructions are also illustrated by schematic drawings and (often) by simple diagrams showing the prescribed folds from a head-on perspective.

Before you begin folding your paper airplane patterns. I would like you to get acquainted with the various graphic symbols printed on the patterns. Each pattern has a top side and a bottom side.

1. Dotted lines indicate fold lines. See the instructions below for making accurate and sharp folds.
2. Dashes or broken lines indicate an area that is to be cut with scissors. Make sure that you hold the two halves of the folded paper plane together firmly before you make your cut. This will ensure that the cut will be even on both sides.
3. Shaded or gray areas indicate sections that must be rubber-cemented together. Use two-coat rubber cement (rubber cement applied to the two surfaces you wish to glue together) and allow enough time for it to dry completely. Then press both sections together firmly. Use a rubber-cement pickup to remove any excess rubber cement.
4. The pattern for Model #7, Gypsy Moth, shows a solid line followed by a dotted line on the underside of both wings. This calls for making a crease at both outer wing tips after you have finished building the plane.

I suggest that you make your first plane of each model using one of the printed patterns. All of the pattern pages are perforated and can be removed from the book by tearing carefully along the perforation. But remember you will not get the best results from folding and flying the pattern page because the paper is not the proper weight. Use the pattern page for practice only. When you have successfully completed your first plane using the printed pattern, you should have no difficulty making others of the same type using appropriate paper of the same size (6″×9″). But if you wish to transfer the numbered folds and cuts of the pattern for each model to another piece of paper, simply remove the second pattern page from the book, lay it beneath the other sheet of paper on any flat, well-lighted surface, like a window pane, and trace the lines and numbers on both sides.

For best results, you will need the following tools and equipment:

1. A sharp pair of scissors, preferably with long, thin blades.
2. A small can of two-coat rubber cement, plus a rubber-cement pickup.
3. Scotch tape.
4. A steel ruler or thin straightedge.
5. A small triangle.
6. A box of medium-sized paper clips.
7. A smooth, flat surface to work on.
8. An X-Acto knife and blades. I recommend using an X-Acto knife (laid along the steel ruler) to cut paper for each model to the desired size. An X-Acto knife, unlike a scissors, ensures a clean, straight cut.

After you have practiced building your first plane using the printed pattern, you will need paper to make additional planes. I recommend 32-pound ledger bond. This is a smooth, firm paper that will enable your plane to withstand a strong throw and maintain its structural integrity in flight. You can buy it (and your other tools and equipment) in an art-supply store (probably not at your local stationer's). The smallest pad is 9″ × 12″; by cutting each page in half (using your X-Acto knife) you will have two sheets of 6″ × 9″, the size I recommend.

A word about folding. Because your airplane must be tightly built and precisely balanced, it is essential that your folds be accurate and sharp. To make a proper fold, lay your steel ruler along the fold line. Then take the paper that extends beyond the ruler and fold it up over the edge of the ruler. Remove the ruler and with your triangle (or thumbnail) sharpen the crease. Always make sure that the edges and corners of facing surfaces meet exactly.

A word, too, about using the X-Acto knife. Make sure to put a magazine or a piece of cardboard underneath the paper you are cutting to prevent damage to your working surface.

Now you are ready to transform a flat, lifeless piece of paper into a sleek, swift, self-stabilizing, stall-resistant paper aircraft.

SKY HAWK

Remove the pattern for the Sky Hawk on pages 99–100 by tearing carefully along the perforation. Then lay the pattern page on a smooth flat surface and follow the step-by-step instructions for this model. But remember, use the pattern page for practice only. You will get the best results when you make your model from the proper paper.

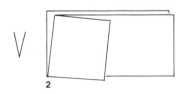

1. Place your ruler on line #1. Lift the paper that extends beyond the ruler and fold it up against the ruler so the crease lies exactly on the printed line. Remove the ruler, complete the fold, and use your triangle (or thumbnail) to sharpen the crease.

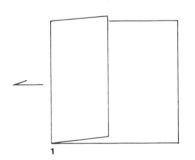

2. Place your ruler on line #2 and then fold, forming the wings of your plane. Make sure the edges and

corners of the wings meet exactly. Sharpen the crease with your triangle or thumbnail.

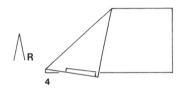

3. Place your ruler on line #3. Fold, then sharpen the crease.

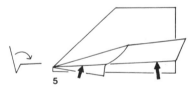

4. Place your ruler on line #4. Fold, then sharpen the crease. These last two folds form the rudder of your airplane. Make sure the edges and corners of the two sides of the rudder meet exactly. With your Scotch tape, tape together the two sides of the rudder that extend beyond line #2.

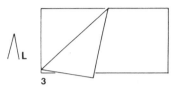

5. Place your ruler on line #5. Lift the wing against the ruler and fold.

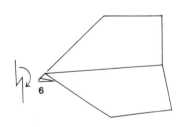

6. Remove the ruler, fold the wing down flat, and sharpen the crease with your triangle or thumbnail.

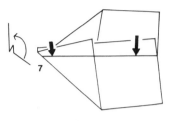

7. Turn the plane over and make fold #6. Remove the ruler, fold the wing down flat, and sharpen the crease. Make sure that the edges and corners of the two wings meet exactly.

8. Place your ruler on line #7. Lift the wing against the ruler and fold.

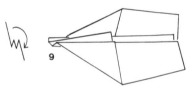

9. Remove the ruler, fold the wing down flat, and sharpen the crease.

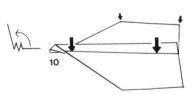

10. Turn the plane over and place your ruler on line #8 (see large arrows). Lift the wing against the ruler and fold. Then remove the ruler, fold the wing down flat, and sharpen the crease. Make sure that the edges and corners of the two wings meet exactly (see small arrows).

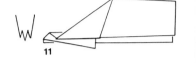

11. Press the plane flat and sharpen all the creases on both sides with your triangle or thumbnail.

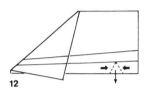

12. Return your plane to its position in instruction (4). With scissors, cut out the notch along line #9. The portion of the fuselage behind the notch will become the plane's tail.

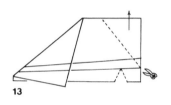

13. Holding the wings firmly together, cut out along line #10.

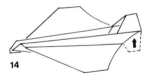

14. Return the plane to its position in instruction (10). Push up the tail section, turning it inside out so it rises above the top of the fuselage. Then recrease the folds on both sides of the tail section.

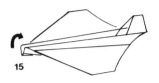

15. Fold the tip of the nose back into the fuselage.

16. Apply two-coat rubber cement to the two inside surfaces of the fuselage and the tail section (the gray areas on the pattern). Allow the rubber cement to dry completely, then press tightly together the inside surfaces of the fuselage and those of the tail section. Use the rubber-cement pickup to remove any excess rubber cement.

17. Return the plane to its position in instruction (13). Cut out a section of the lower fuselage along line #11.

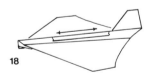

18. Place Scotch tape along the seam of the fuselage, leaving enough room to insert a paper clip in the forward portion. (The Scotch tape will hold the fuselage firmly together.)

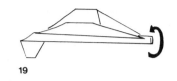

19. Holding the plane upside down, squeeze the front of the fuselage together, then wrap Scotch tape around the nose several times. Trim off all excess tape.

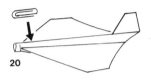

20. Turn the plane rightside up and insert a paper clip (for weight) into the front section of the fuselage.

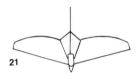

21. Straighten the wings. Your plane is now ready to fly. To ensure a perfect flight, read the section "How to Fine-Tune Your Paper Plane" on pages 84–88.

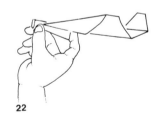

22. To launch your plane, hold its nose between your thumb and middle finger. Place your index finger behind the rudder. Throw the plane into the wind, hard and straight, like throwing a ball.

SUPER HAWK

Remove the pattern for the Super Hawk on pages 103–104 by tearing carefully along the perforation. Then lay the pattern page on a smooth flat surface and follow the step-by-step instructions for this model. But remember, use the pattern page for practice only. You will get the best results when you make your model from the proper paper.

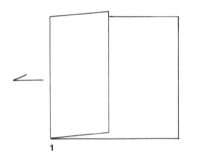

1. Place your ruler on line #1. Lift the paper that extends beyond the ruler and fold it up against the ruler so the crease lies exactly on the printed line. Remove the ruler, complete the fold, and use your triangle (or thumbnail) to sharpen the crease.

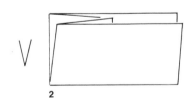

2. Place your ruler on line #2 and then fold, forming the wings of your plane. Make sure that the edges and corners of the wings meet exactly. Sharpen the crease with your triangle or thumbnail.

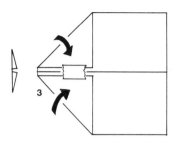

3. Return the plane to its position in instruction (1). Place your ruler on line #3. Fold, then sharpen the crease. Place your ruler on line #4. Fold, then sharpen the crease. Holding the two triangular pieces flat, tape them together.

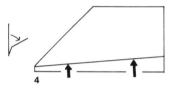

4. Refold the wings along line #2. Then place your ruler on line #5.

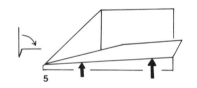

5. Lift the wing against the ruler and fold.

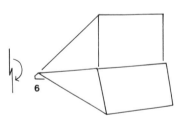

6. Remove the ruler and fold the wing down flat, sharpening the crease with your triangle or thumbnail.

7. Turn the plane over. Place your ruler on line #6. Lift the wing against the ruler and fold.

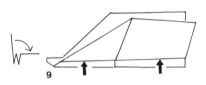

8. Remove the ruler and fold the wing down flat, then sharpen the crease with your triangle or thumbnail. Make sure that the edges and corners of the two wings meet exactly.

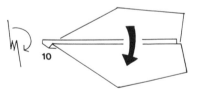

9. Place your ruler on line #7. Fold the wing up against the ruler.

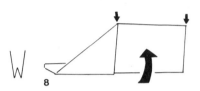

10. Remove the ruler and fold the wing down flat, sharpening the crease with your triangle or thumbnail.

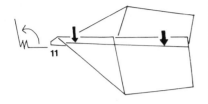

11. Turn the plane over. Place your ruler on line #8. Fold the wing up against the ruler.

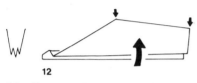

12. Remove the ruler and fold the wing down flat, sharpening the crease with your triangle or thumbnail. Make sure that the edges and corners of the two wings meet exactly. Now, press the plane flat and sharpen all the creases on both sides with your triangle or thumbnail.

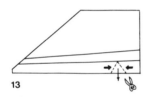

13. Return the plane to its position in instruction (4). With your scissors, cut out the notch along line #9. The portion of the fuselage in front of the notch will become the plane's rudder, the portion behind the notch will become the plane's tail.

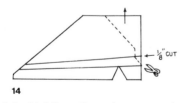

14. Holding the wings together firmly, cut out along line #10. Make cuts ⅛" long on lines #7 and #8.

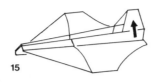

15. Return the plane to its position in instruction (11). Push up the tail section, turning it inside out so it rises above the top of the fuselage. Now recrease the folds on both sides of the tail section.

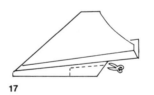

16. Next, fold the tip of the nose back into the fuselage. Apply two-coat rubber cement to the two inside surfaces of the fuselage and the tail section (the gray area on the pattern). Allow the rubber cement to dry completely, then press tightly together the inside surfaces of the fuselage and those of the tail section. Use the rubber-cement pickup to remove any excess rubber cement.

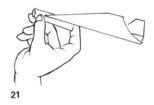

17. With the wings folded up in the position shown in instruction (13), cut out a section of the rudder along line #11.

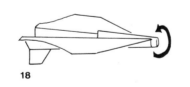

18. Holding the plane upside down, squeeze the front of the fuselage together, then wrap Scotch tape around the nose several times. Trim off all excess tape.

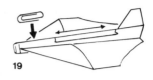

19. Insert a paper clip (for weight) into the front of the fuselage, then place Scotch tape along the seam of the fuselage to reinforce.

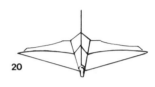

20. Straighten the wings. Your plane is now ready to fly. To ensure a perfect flight, read the section "How to Fine-Tune Your Paper Plane" on pages 84–88.

21. To launch your plane, hold its nose between your thumb and middle finger. Place your index finger behind the rudder. Throw the plane into the wind, hard and straight, like throwing a ball.

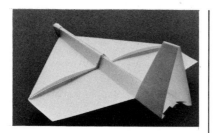

VOYAGER

Remove the pattern for the Voyager on pages 107–108 by tearing carefully along the perforation. Then lay the pattern page on a smooth flat surface and follow the step-by-step instructions for this model. But remember, use the pattern page for practice only. You will get the best results when you make your model from the proper paper.

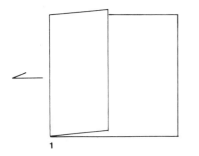

1. Place your ruler on line #1. Lift the paper that extends beyond the ruler and fold it up against the ruler so the crease lies exactly on the printed line. Remove the ruler, complete the fold, and use your triangle (or thumbnail) to sharpen the crease.

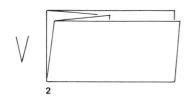

2. Place your ruler on line #2 and then fold, forming the wings of your plane. Make sure that the edges and corners of the wings meet exactly. Sharpen the crease with your triangle or thumbnail.

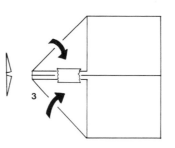

3. Return the plane to its position in instruction (1). Place your ruler on line #3. Fold, then sharpen the crease. Place your ruler on line #4. Fold, then sharpen the crease. Holding the two triangular pieces flat, tape them together.

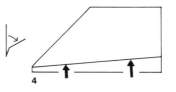

4. Refold the wings along line #2. Then place your ruler on line #5.

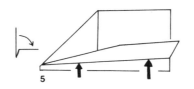

5. Lift the wing against the ruler and fold.

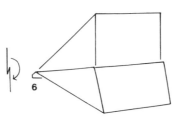

6. Remove the ruler and fold the wing down flat, sharpening the crease with your triangle or thumbnail.

7. Turn the plane over. Place your ruler on line #6. Lift the wing against the ruler and fold.

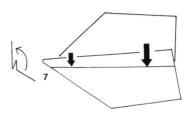

8. Remove the ruler and fold the wing down flat, then sharpen the crease with your triangle or thumbnail. Make sure that the edges and corners of the two wings meet exactly.

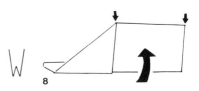

9. Place your ruler on line #7. Fold the wing up against the ruler.

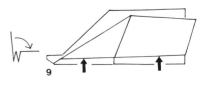

10. Remove the ruler and fold the wing down flat, sharpening the crease with your triangle or thumbnail.

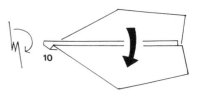

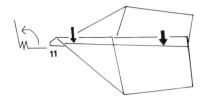

11. Turn the plane over. Place your ruler on line #8. Fold the wing up against the ruler.

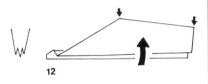

12. Remove the ruler and fold the wing down flat, sharpening the crease with your triangle or thumbnail. Make sure that the edges and corners of the two wings meet exactly. Press the plane flat and sharpen all the creases on both sides with your triangle or thumbnail.

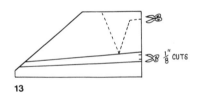

13. Return the plane to its position in instruction (4). Holding the wings together firmly, cut out along line #9. Then make ⅛" cuts on the two dashed lines at the rear of the fuselage.

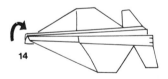

14. Return the plane to its position in instruction (12). Now fold the tip of the nose back into the fuselage.

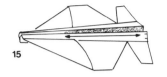

15. Apply two-coat rubber cement to the two inside surfaces of the fuselage (the gray area on the pattern). Allow the rubber cement to dry completely, then press tightly together the two inside surfaces of the fuselage. Use the rubber-cement pickup to remove any excess rubber cement.

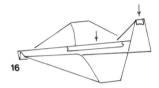

16. Scotch tape the seam of the fuselage, leaving room for a paper clip in the forward section. This will reinforce the fuselage. Now fold up the two sides of the tail section and recrease folds. Line up the tops of the tail sections exactly, and tape them together. Trim off any excess tape.

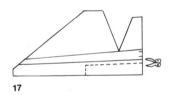

17. With the wings folded up in the position shown in instruction (13), cut out along line #10, forming the plane's rudder.

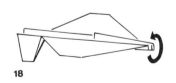

18. Holding the plane upside down, squeeze the front of the fuselage together, then wrap Scotch tape around the nose several times. Trim off all excess tape.

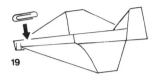

19. Insert a paper clip (for weight) into the front section of the fuselage.

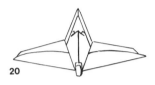

20. Straighten the wings. Your plane is now ready to fly. To ensure a perfect flight, read the section "How to Fine-Tune Your Paper Plane" on pages 84–88.

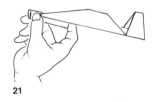

21. To launch your plane, hold its nose between your thumb and middle finger. Place your index finger behind the rudder. Throw the plane into the wind, hard and straight, like throwing a ball.

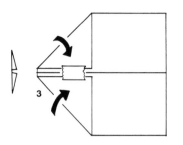

CONDOR

Remove the pattern for the Condor on pages 111–112 by tearing carefully along the perforation. Then lay the pattern page on a smooth flat surface and follow the step-by-step instructions for this model. But remember, use the pattern page for practice only. You will get the best results when you make your model from the proper paper.

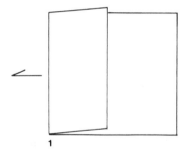

1. Place your ruler on line #1. Lift the paper that extends beyond the ruler and fold it up against the ruler so the crease lies exactly on the printed line. Remove the ruler, complete the fold, and use your triangle (or thumbnail) to sharpen the crease.

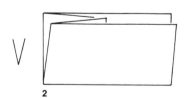

2. Place your ruler on line #2 and then fold, forming the wings of your plane. Make sure that the edges and corners of the wings meet exactly. Sharpen the crease with your triangle or thumbnail.

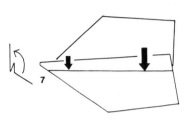

3. Return the plane to its position in instruction (1). Place your ruler on line #3. Fold, then sharpen the crease. Place your ruler on line #4. Fold, then sharpen the crease. Holding the two triangular pieces flat, tape them together.

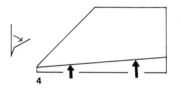

4. Refold the wings along line #2. Then place your ruler on line #5.

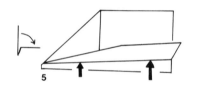

5. Lift the wing against the ruler and fold.

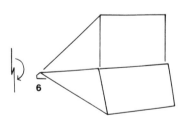

6. Remove the ruler and fold the wing down flat, sharpening the crease with your triangle or thumbnail.

7. Turn the plane over. Place your ruler on line #6. Lift the wing against the ruler and fold.

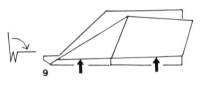

8. Remove the ruler and fold the wing down flat, then sharpen the crease with your triangle or thumbnail. Make sure that the edges and corners of the two wings meet exactly.

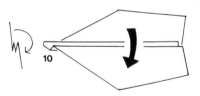

9. Place your ruler on line #7. Fold the wing up against the ruler.

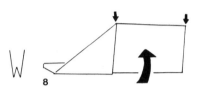

10. Remove the ruler and fold the wing down flat, sharpening the crease with your triangle or thumbnail.

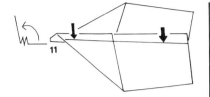

11. Turn the plane over. Place your ruler on line #8. Fold the wing up against the ruler.

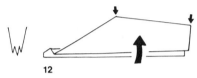

12. Remove the ruler and fold the wing down flat, sharpening the crease with your triangle or thumbnail. Make sure that the edges and corners of the two wings meet exactly. Press the plane flat and sharpen all the creases on both sides with your triangle or thumbnail.

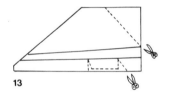

13. Return the plane to its position in instruction (4). With your scissors, cut out along line #9, forming the tail section (rear), rudder (front), and stabilizers (center). Then, holding the wings firmly together, cut along line #10.

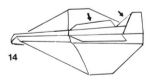

14. Push up the tail section, turning it inside out so it rises above the top of the fuselage. Recrease the folds on both sides of the tail section. Now, push up the stabilizers in the same way and refold them so they extend upward on each side of the plane.

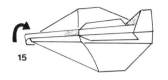

15. Now fold the tip of the plane's nose back into the fuselage. Apply two-coat rubber cement to the two inside surfaces of the fuselage and the tail section (the gray areas on the pattern). Allow the rubber cement to dry completely, then press tightly together the inside surfaces of the fuselage and those of the tail section. Use the rubber-cement pickup to remove any excess rubber cement.

16. Turn the plane upside down and tape the seam of the fuselage its full length behind the rudder. The tape will reinforce the seam.

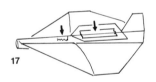

17. Turn the plane rightside up. Tape the seam between the stabilizers. Also tape the seam on the upper fuselage, but leave room for a paper clip to be inserted in the front of the fuselage.

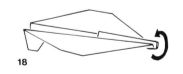

18. Holding the plane upside down, squeeze the front of the fuselage together, then wrap Scotch tape around the nose several times. Trim off all excess tape.

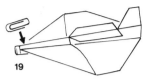

19. Insert a paper clip (for weight) into the front of the fuselage.

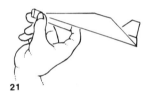

20. Straighten the wings. Your plane is now ready to fly. To ensure a perfect flight, read the section "How to Fine-Tune Your Paper Plane" on pages 84–88.

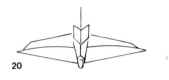

21. To launch your plane, hold its nose between your thumb and middle finger. Place your index finger behind the rudder. Throw the plane into the wind, hard and straight, like throwing a ball.

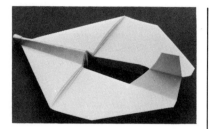

GYRFALCON

Remove the pattern for the Gyrfalcon on pages 115–116 by tearing carefully along the perforation. Then lay the pattern page on a smooth flat surface and follow the step-by-step instructions for this model. But remember, use the pattern page for practice only. You will get the best results when you make your model from the proper paper.

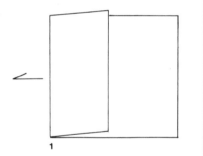

1. Place your ruler on line #1. Lift the paper that extends beyond the ruler and fold it up against the ruler so the crease lies exactly on the printed line. Remove the ruler, complete the fold, and use your triangle (or thumbnail) to sharpen the crease.

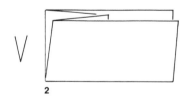

2. Place your ruler on line #2 and then fold, forming the wings of your plane. Make sure that the edges and the corners of the wings meet exactly. Sharpen the crease with your triangle or thumbnail.

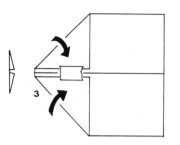

3. Return the plane to its position in instruction (1). Place your ruler on line #3. Fold, then sharpen the crease. Place your ruler on line #4. Fold, then sharpen the crease. Holding the two triangular pieces flat, tape them together.

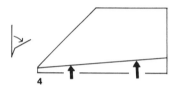

4. Refold the wings along line #2. Then place your ruler on line #5.

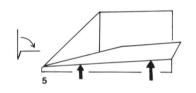

5. Lift the wing against the ruler and fold.

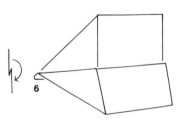

6. Remove the ruler and fold the wing down flat, sharpening the crease with your triangle or thumbnail.

7. Turn the plane over. Place your ruler on line #6. Lift the wing against the ruler and fold.

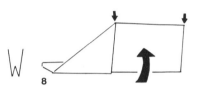

8. Remove the ruler and fold the wing down flat, then sharpen the crease with your triangle or thumbnail. Make sure that the edges and corners of the two wings meet exactly.

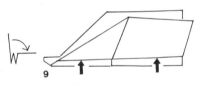

9. Place your ruler on line #7. Fold the wing up against the ruler.

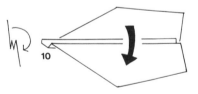

10. Remove the ruler and fold the wing down flat, sharpening the crease with your triangle or thumbnail.

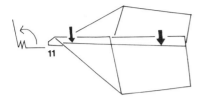

11. Turn the plane over. Place your ruler on line #8. Fold the wing up against the ruler.

12. Remove the ruler and fold the wing down flat, sharpening the crease with your triangle or thumbnail. Make sure that the edges and corners of the two wings meet exactly.

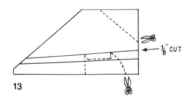

13. Return the plane to its position in instruction (4). With your scissors, cut out along line #9, forming the tail section (rear), rudder (front), and landing gear (center). Then, holding the wings firmly together, cut out along line #10. Finally, make a ⅛" cut in the tail section to form the flaps that will provide reflex action.

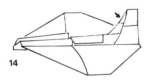

14. Push up the tail section, turning it inside out so it rises above the top of the fuselage. Recrease the folds on both sides of the tail section.

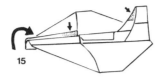

15. Next, fold the tip of the plane's nose back into the fuselage. Apply two-coat rubber cement to the two inside surfaces of the fuselage and the tail section (the gray areas on the pattern). Allow the rubber cement to dry completely, then press tightly together the inside surfaces of the fuselage and those of the tail section. Use the rubber-cement pickup to remove any excess rubber cement.

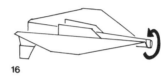

16. Holding the plane upside down, squeeze the front of the fuselage together, then wrap Scotch tape around the nose several times. Trim off all excess tape.

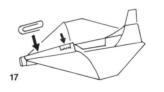

17. Holding the plane rightside up, insert a paper clip (for weight) into the front of the fuselage. Then tape the seam of the fuselage behind the paper clip. Also tape the seam on the underside of the fuselage where the tail section is joined together. This tape will reinforce the seams.

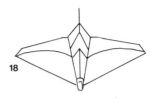

18. Straighten the wings, making sure that the rear portions of the wings curve upward. Open the flaps slightly. See that the landing gears extend down and slightly outward at the same angle. Your plane is now ready to fly. To ensure a perfect flight, read the section "How to Fine-Tune Your Paper Plane" on pages 84–88.

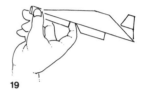

19. To launch your plane, hold its nose between your thumb and middle finger. Place your index finger behind the rudder. Do not throw this plane hard. Give it a gentle throw into the wind.

STING RAY

Remove the pattern for the Sting Ray on pages 119–120 by tearing carefully along the perforation. Then lay the pattern page on a smooth flat surface and follow the step-by-step instructions for this model. But remember, use the pattern page for practice only. You will get the best results when you make your model from the proper paper.

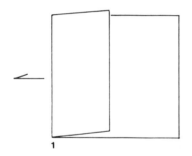

1. Place your ruler on line #1. Lift the paper that extends beyond the ruler and fold it up against the ruler so the crease lies exactly on the printed line. Remove the ruler, complete the fold, and use your triangle (or thumbnail) to sharpen the crease.

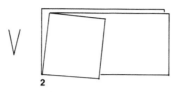

2. Place your ruler on line #2 and then fold, forming the wings of your plane. Make sure that the edges and corners of the wings meet exactly. Sharpen the crease with your triangle or thumbnail.

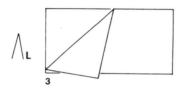

3. Place your ruler on line #3. Fold, then sharpen the crease.

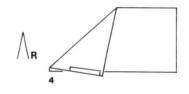

4. Place your ruler on line #4. Fold, then sharpen the crease. These last two folds form the rudder of your airplane. Make sure the edges and corners of the two sides of the rudder meet exactly. With your Scotch tape, tape together the two sides of the rudder that extend beyond line #2.

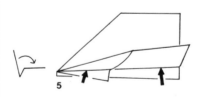

5. Place your ruler on line #5. Lift the wing against the ruler and fold.

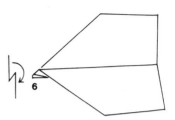

6. Remove the ruler, fold the wing down flat, and sharpen the crease with your triangle or thumbnail.

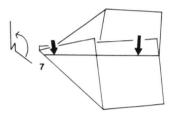

7. Turn the plane over and make fold #6. Remove the ruler, fold the wing down flat, and sharpen the crease. Make sure that the edges and corners of the two wings meet exactly.

8. Place your ruler on line #7. Lift the wing against the ruler and fold.

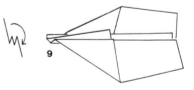

9. Remove the ruler, fold the wing down flat, and sharpen the crease.

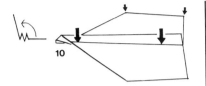

10. Turn the plane over and place your ruler on line #8 (see large arrows). Lift the wing against the ruler and fold. Then remove the ruler, fold the wing down flat, and sharpen the crease. Make sure that the edges and corners of the two wings meet exactly (see small arrows).

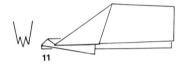

11. Press the plane flat and sharpen all the creases on both sides with your triangle or thumbnail.

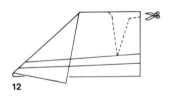

12. Return your plane to its position in instruction (4). Holding the wings firmly together, cut out along line #9.

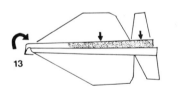

13. Now fold the tip of the nose back into the fuselage. Apply two-coat rubber cement to the two inside surfaces of the fuselage (the gray area on the pattern), leaving room for a paper clip to be inserted in the front of the fuselage. Allow the rubber cement to dry completely, then press tightly together the two inside surfaces of the fuselage. Use the rubber-cement pickup to remove any excess rubber cement.

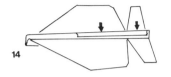

14. Tape the seam of the fuselage, still leaving room for a paper clip at the front.

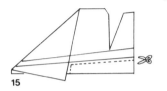

15. Return the plane to its position in instruction (12). Cut out a section of the lower fuselage along line #10.

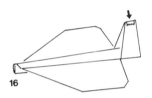

16. Bring the two sides of the tail section together, line them up exactly, and tape them together at the top. Trim off excess tape.

17. Holding the plane upside down, squeeze the front of the fuselage together, then wrap Scotch tape around the nose several times. Trim off all excess tape.

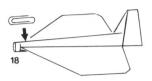

18. Insert a paper clip (for weight) into the forward portion of the fuselage.

19. Straighten the wings. Your plane is now ready to fly. To ensure a perfect flight, read the section "How to Fine-Tune Your Paper Plane" on pages 84–88.

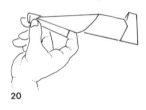

20. To launch your plane, hold its nose between your thumb and middle finger. Place your index finger behind the rudder. Throw the plane into the wind, hard and straight, like throwing a ball.

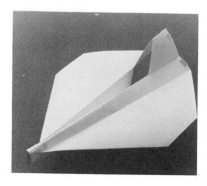

GYPSY MOTH

Remove the pattern for the Gypsy Moth on pages 123–124 by tearing carefully along the perforation. Then lay the pattern page on a smooth flat surface and follow the step-by-step instructions for this model. But remember, use the pattern page for practice only. You will get the best results when you make your model from the proper paper.

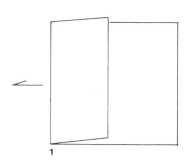

1. Place your ruler on line #1. Lift the paper that extends beyond the ruler and fold it up against the ruler so the crease lies exactly on the printed line. Remove the ruler, complete the fold, and use your triangle (or thumbnail) to sharpen the crease.

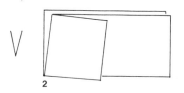

2. Place your ruler on line #2 and then fold, forming the wings of your plane. Make sure that the edges and corners of the wings meet exactly. Sharpen the crease with your triangle or thumbnail.

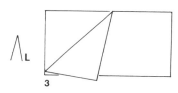

3. Place your ruler on line #3. Fold, then sharpen the crease.

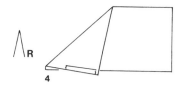

4. Place your ruler on line #4. Fold, then sharpen the crease. These last two folds form the rudder of your airplane. Make sure the edges and corners of the two sides of the rudder meet exactly. With your Scotch tape, tape together the two sides of the rudder that extend beyond line #2.

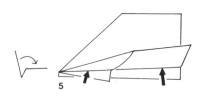

5. Place your ruler on line #5. Lift the wing against the ruler and fold.

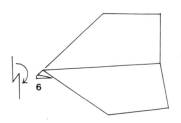

6. Remove the ruler, fold the wing down flat, and sharpen the crease with your triangle or thumbnail.

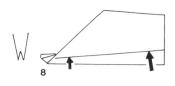

7. Turn the plane over and make fold #6. Remove the ruler, fold the wing down flat, and sharpen the crease. Make sure that the edges and corners of the two wings meet exactly.

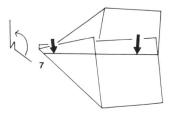

8. Place your ruler on line #7. Lift the wing against the ruler and fold.

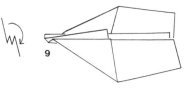

9. Remove the ruler, fold the wing down flat, and sharpen the crease.

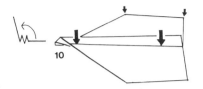

10. Turn the plane over and place your ruler on line #8 (see large arrows). Lift the wing against the ruler and fold. Then remove the ruler, fold the wing down flat, and sharpen the crease. Make sure that the edges and corners of the two wings meet exactly (see small arrows).

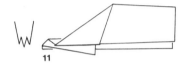

11. Press the plane flat and sharpen all the creases on both sides with your triangle or thumbnail.

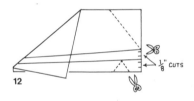

12. Return your plane to its position in instruction (4). With your scissors, cut out the notch along line #9. The portion of the fuselage behind the notch will become the plane's tail section. Holding the wings firmly together, cut out along line #10. Then make ⅛" cuts on the dashed lines on the rear fuselage. These will form flaps that will make the plane climb and turn.

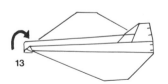

13. Fold the tip of the plane's nose back into the fuselage.

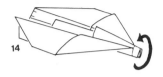

14. Holding the plane upside down, squeeze the front of the fuselage together, then wrap Scotch tape around the nose several times. Trim off all excess tape.

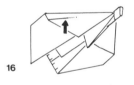

15. Holding the plane rightside up, push the lower section of the left wing forward about ³⁄₁₆" at the wing's outer edge (along line #11). Pinch a crease on line #11.

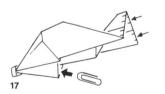

16. Similarly, push the lower section of the right wing forward about ³⁄₁₆" at the wing's outer edge (along line #12). Pinch a crease on line #12.

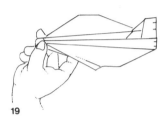

17. Place a paper clip (for weight) inside the rudder and tape rear end of the rudder shut. Then gently open one set of flaps in the tail section. This will make the plane loop. If you want the plane to turn to the right, open the right flap in the fuselage. To make the plane turn to the left, open the left flap in the fuselage.

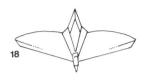

18. Straighten the wings. Your plane is now ready to fly. To ensure a perfect flight, read the section "How to Fine-Tune Your Paper Plane" on pages 84–88.

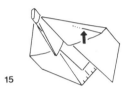

19. To launch your plane, hold its nose between your thumb and middle finger. Place your index finger behind the rudder. Throw the plane into the wind, hard and straight, like throwing a ball.

How to Fine-Tune Your Paper Plane

After you have finished making your paper plane, you should take a moment to study it head-on. What you want to look for is uniformity on both sides of the fuselage. Both wings should be of the same thickness and line up with the fuselage at the same angle. The reason for this is simple. If you want the plane to fly perfectly straight, which it is capable of doing when properly balanced, the air must pass over the same wing area on both sides to maintain a neutral direction. If the plane is *not* equal on both sides, that will definitely affect the line of flight.

Again, check the plane head-on. If one wing appears larger than the other, recrease the larger wing with your fingers until you have reduced the size to that of the opposite wing. If you notice that the crease that connects the fuselage to the wing is higher on one side than the other, try twisting the fuselage slightly, until both sides are the same. Also check the tail section to make sure that it is straight. You can press the underside of each wing upward where it has been taped to the fuselage to make sure that it meets the air at the correct angle of attack. In addition, check the outer wing tips on both sides to make sure they are at the same angle. The wings on all models do not require any dihedral or slight angle upward extending outward from the fuselage. The wings should come out straight from the fuselage on both sides. If you have followed these suggestions, you are now ready for your first test flight. Let 'er rip!

This diagram represents the various sections of the models (#1, #6, and #7) that have the step on the bottom. They do not require a reflex action, but if flaps are added to the trailing edge of the fuselage they will climb more sharply.

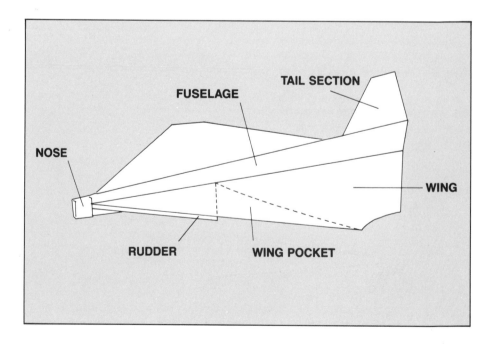

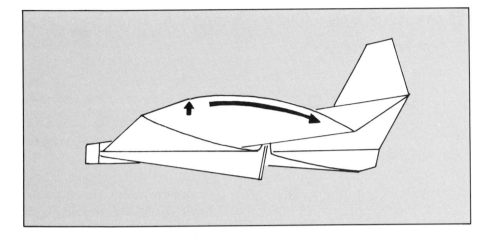

Carefully study the arrows in this illustration. The wing tips (small arrow) should always be up straight, never bent downward. The trailing edge of the wing (large, curved arrow) should always be arched slightly upward, as shown.

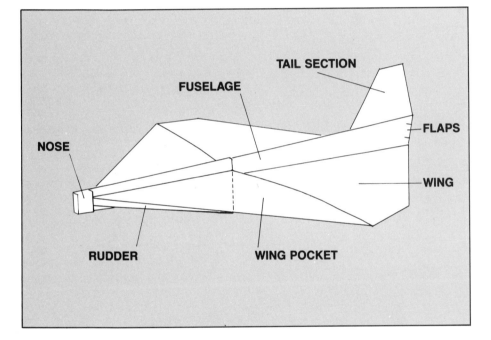

This diagram illustrates the various sections of the models (#2, #3, #4, and #5) that have the step on the top. They *all* require a reflex action, which can be achieved by cutting flaps into the trailing edge of the fuselage. The Condor, model #4, has a pair of stabilizers on the top of the fuselage. Additional reflex can be added, if necessary, by turning the trailing edge of each stabilizer slightly upward or by cutting flaps into the trailing edge of the fuselage.

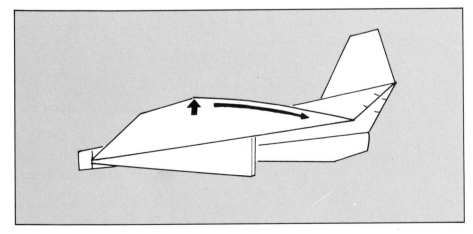

Carefully study the arrows indicated in this illustration. The wing tips (small arrow) should always be straight, never bent downward. The trailing edge of the wing (large, curved arrow) should always be arched slightly upward, as shown.

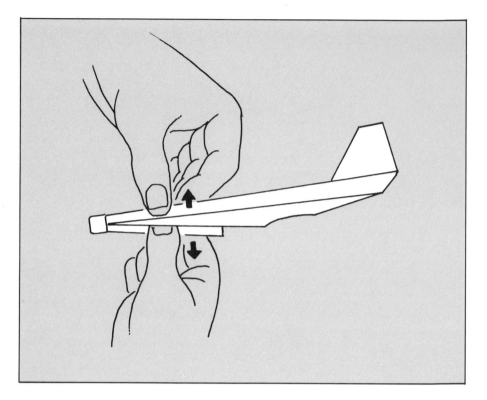

If your plane (models #1, #6, or #7) does not achieve sufficient lift, hold the fuselage with one hand (as shown), hold the rudder with your other hand, and pull both sections apart slightly. Then check your plane head-on to make sure that both wings are equal in size.

It is important to examine the paper plane from the tail section to determine whether or not the trailing edges of both wings are at the same angle. If your plane is going to fly straight, it must be symmetrical. If one wing is higher than the other at the trailing edge (see arrow), it will affect the line of flight. Try twisting the body of the plane until both points line up as shown.

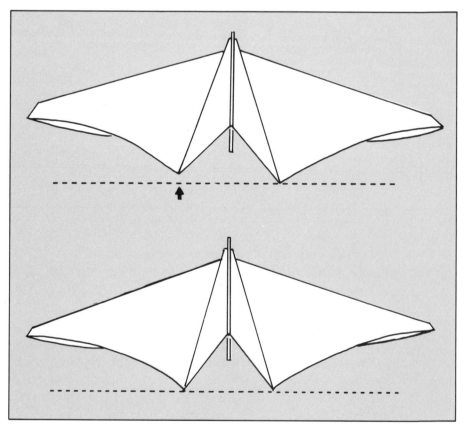

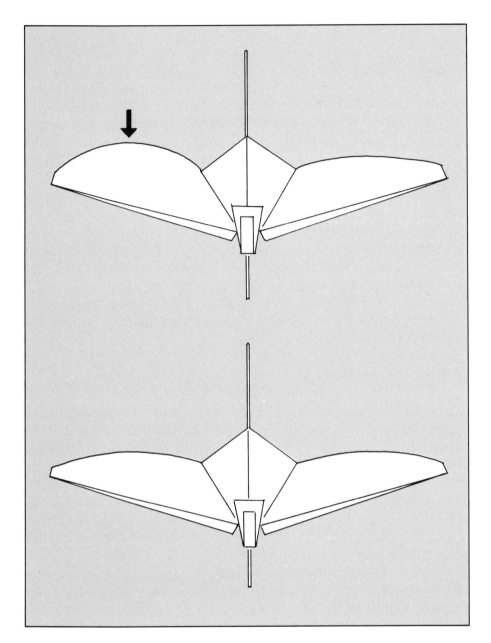

It is important to examine the paper plane head-on (as shown) to determine that the size of both wing pockets is the same as well as at the same angle of attack where the wings meet the fuselage. If your plane is going to fly straight, it must be symmetrical. If one wing is larger than the other (see arrow), you must reduce the size of that wing until both wings are the same. Recrease the larger pocket with your finger tips, pushing the leading edge upward as you move your fingers from root to wing tip.

Hopefully all went well. But if you experienced a problem, check the illustrations and captions here and on the preceding three pages. Also check the following list for the possible solution.

1. Does the plane develop enough lift?

Perhaps you are not throwing the plane hard enough. If it took a nosedive, try throwing it with more force. If the plane sinks too rapidly, try increasing the pockets in the wings slightly. You can do this as follows: Hold the rudder with one hand. Then take hold of the fuselage on the opposite side with your other hand. Now pull the two sections apart slightly. If you pull them too far apart, just push them together. Now make another test flight. The wings should now produce sufficient lift.

2. Does the plane climb too quickly?

If so, make sure that you have inserted a paper clip in the nose, because the plane needs forward weight to carry it ahead. If it still climbs too sharply, you will have to reduce the depth of the pockets in both wings, because they are producing too much lift. Try recreasing both wings, starting at the leading edges, with your fingers. As you run your fingers along the leading edges, try giving the wings' undersides a twist upward. This should help to reduce the size of the pockets. Or you might try folding the plane up completely, if it is one of the models with the step on the bottom. Recrease all the folds, then straighten the wings out once again. Check it head-on for proper alignment. Then throw it. This method of folding the plane up completely is also good for transporting a number of planes to the local park or ball field.

3. Does the plane veer off to the left or right sharply?

If so, something is out of alignment. First, check the angle of attack on both wings. Do they meet at the exact same position on both sides of the fuselage? If not, you have a problem in the angle of attack, which occurred in the folding. Either try to correct the folds so that they both meet exactly or start over. Next check the alignment of the plane head-on. If one wing appears to be larger than the other, the larger wing is producing more resistance to the air and will definitely affect the line of flight by causing the plane to turn. Either reduce the size of the larger pocket or increase the size of the smaller pocket until they are identical.

Next, examine the creases on both sides where the wing meets the fuselage. If one side is higher than the other, try twisting the fuselage slightly until both sides are at the same angle. An improper alignment of the fuselage and wing will definitely affect the line of flight. Remember, you are seeking a perfectly straight flight path. Also check the tail section and rudder to make sure they are straight. A head-on examination will usually tell you what you need to know.

If you still experience a problem, try giving a more gentle, upward curve to the trailing edge of the wing that is *not* providing enough lift.

These instructions should cover most situations regarding the flight path. If nothing seems to work, it may be something that you are unable to detect. It is better to start over again. The next model will more than likely perform as it was designed to do.

Special Instructions for Fine-Tuning Your Plane with the Step on Top

The natural tendency of the Kline-Fogleman airfoil is to fly with the step on the bottom without needing a reflex action. When the step is placed on the top, however, it will provide much more lift but it will also require a *reflex action*. It can be a tricky airplane to make because of this tendency. If it is made correctly, you should not have any difficulty getting spectacular flights. But it is important to understand the airfoil's characteristics in order to master it.

The bottom wing area should always be sloped upward from front to back. In addition, the stabilizers on both sides of the fuselage at the tail section must always be angled upward so they provide the necessary reflex action. Do not allow the pockets in the wings to get too large, because they will require more reflex than is necessary.

When made correctly, models with the step on top should easily be able to climb higher than the average telephone pole—providing, of course, you give it a strong throw into the wind. Also try throwing your plane on a slight angle, with the right wing a bit lower than the left. This will cause the plane to climb up on an angle into the wind. When it reaches the apogee, it will then level off and go into a beautiful, long glide. Since the plane is self-stabilizing, it is very easy to achieve this maneuver. Always give the plane a strong throw.

A Few Words About Weather Conditions

Weather conditions can have an effect on your paper plane. Your paper plane will be subject to the moisture in the air, which causes the paper to warp slightly in various ways. More than likely, you will test-fly and fine-tune your new plane in the house first. But once you take the plane outside, humidity may come into play. If the weather is dry, there should be no problem. If there is a light breeze, you should experience some great flights. However, if there is a lot of moisture in the air, you are likely to run into problems. You will have to periodically retune the plane. If it is drizzling or raining, forget it altogether. It's a washout.

A very windy day will also affect your flights, because the Kline-Fogleman airfoil has a natural tendency to turn nose forward into the wind and stabilize. The plane wants to fly level with the earth at all times.

So you will have to experiment and experience for yourself when weather conditions are most suitable for your flights. If you are lucky enough to have a large indoor area, then you have the perfect place for perfect flights every time. Outside, there are many more variables. And, of course, even apparently identical versions of all seven models of the Ultimate Paper Airplane do not fly the same way every time. That is where the real fun comes in. Similar models can be pitted against each other, or against different models, in contests for distance, altitude, maneuverability, and anything else you can think of.

Let the competition begin.

Patterns for the Ultimate Paper Airplane

Two patterns for each model of the Ultimate Paper Airplane are printed on the following pages. The pages are perforated and can be removed from the book by tearing carefully along the perforation. Make your first plane of each model using one of the printed patterns. Remove it from the book and then follow the step-by-step instructions for that model. The second of the two printed patterns can be used to transfer the numbered folds and cuts of the pattern to paper of the proper weight. Remove the pattern page from the book and lay it beneath the other sheet of paper on any flat, well-lighted surface, like a windowpane, and trace the lines and numbers on both sides.

Once you have mastered the art of folding and flying these models of the Ultimate Paper Airplane, your creations will give you many hours of fun. But that could be just the beginning. You may want to experiment by varying the basic design of each model and testing its characteristics in flight. You may even invent a model that will be uniquely your own. Onward and upward. And may you attain the perfect flight.

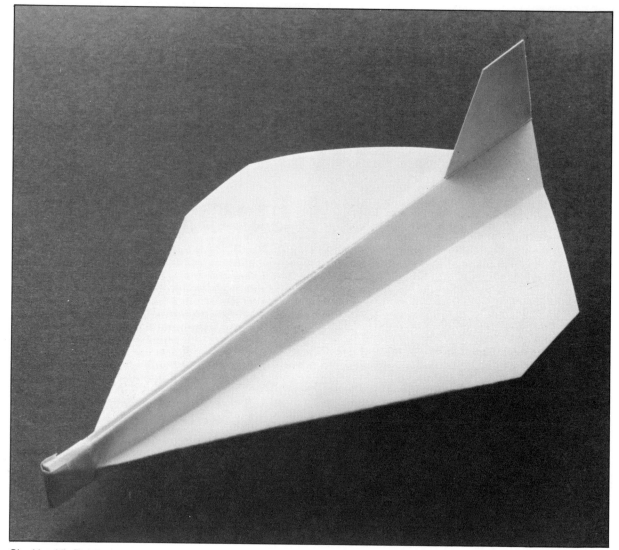

Sky Hawk's flight
characteristics of self-
stabilizing and resistance
to stalling make it unique
among paper airplanes.

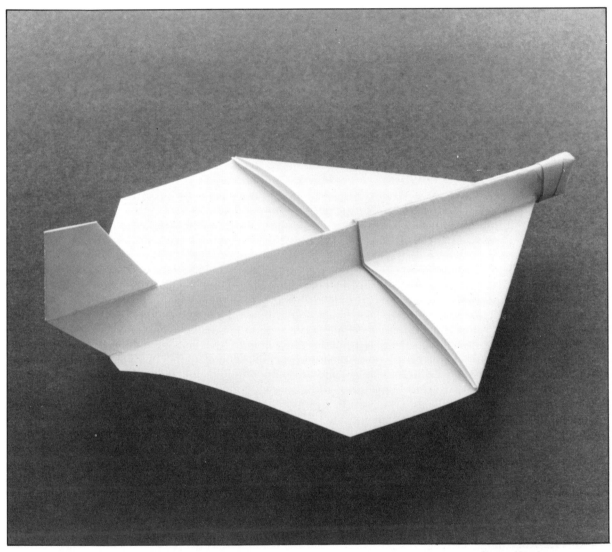

Super Hawk, an
improvement over the
original design, will climb
much higher than Sky
Hawk.

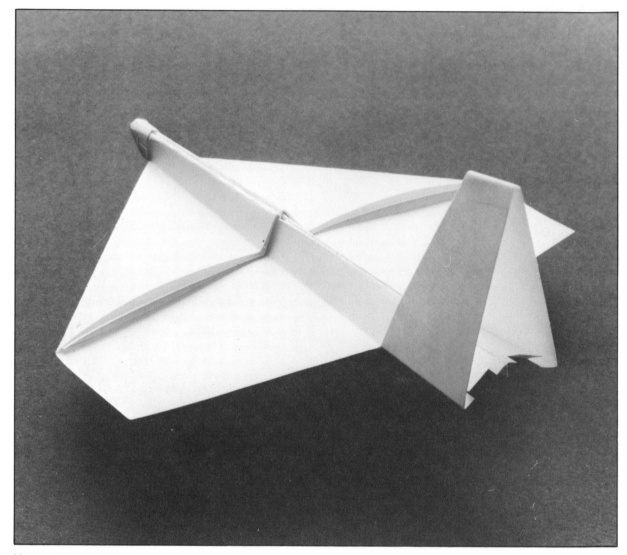

Voyager, a variation of
Super Hawk, will achieve
greater distance every
time.

Condor is perhaps the most sophisticated, high-performance model of them all.

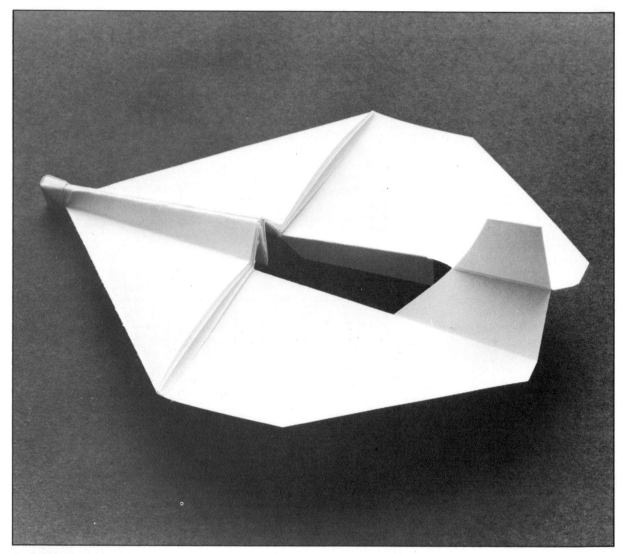

Gyrfalcon is designed for
gentle flights and smooth
landings.

Sting Ray, a variation of
Sky Hawk, is notable for
high looping flights.

Gypsy Moth is a superb
aerial acrobat.

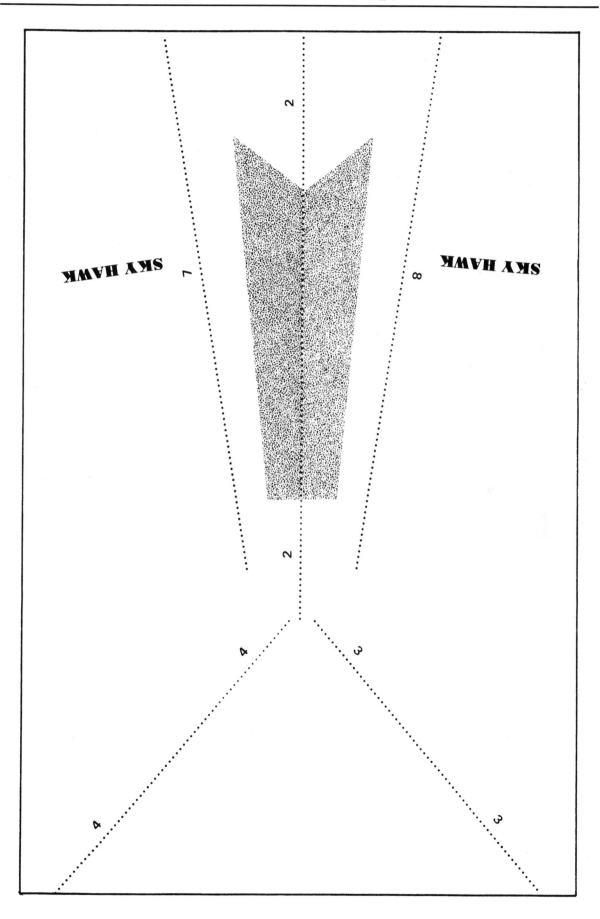

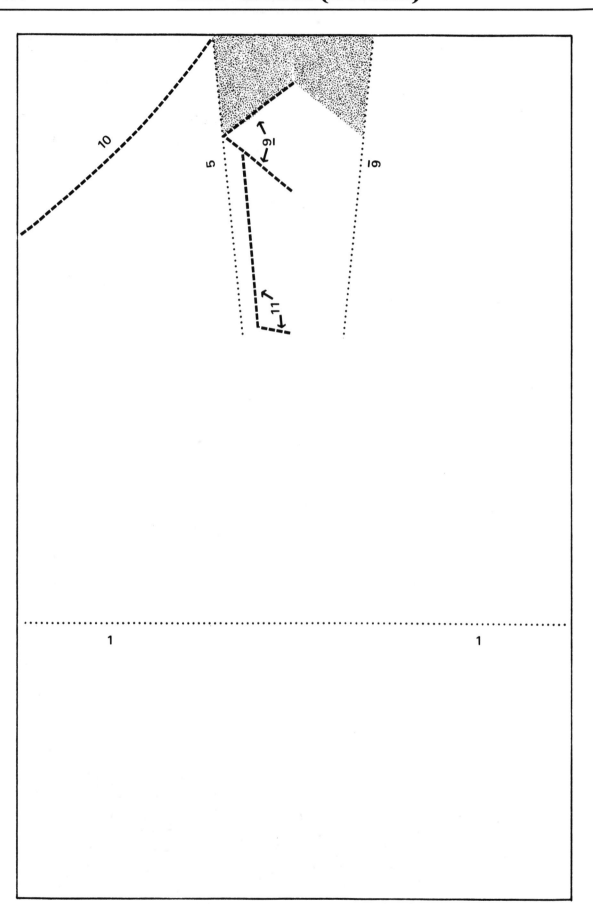

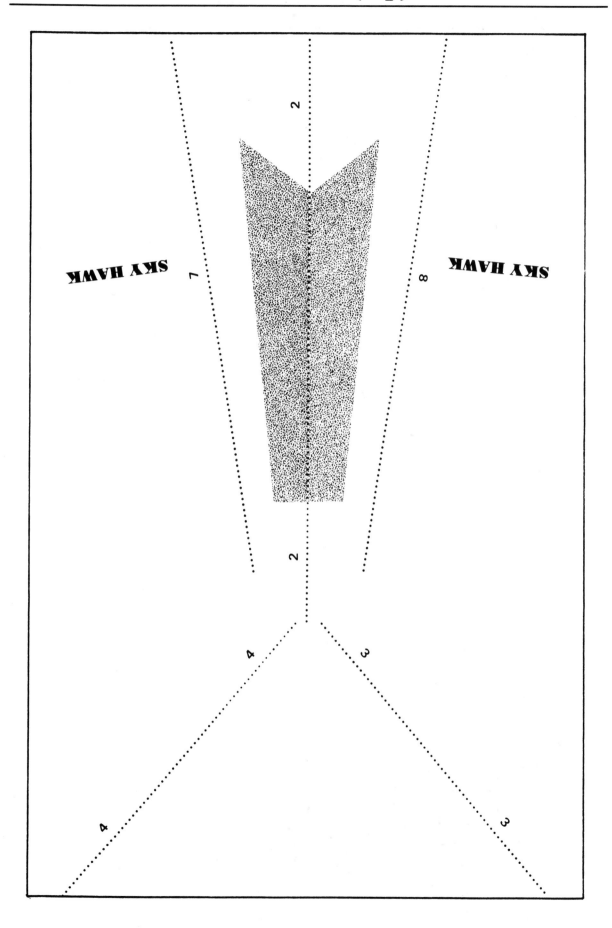

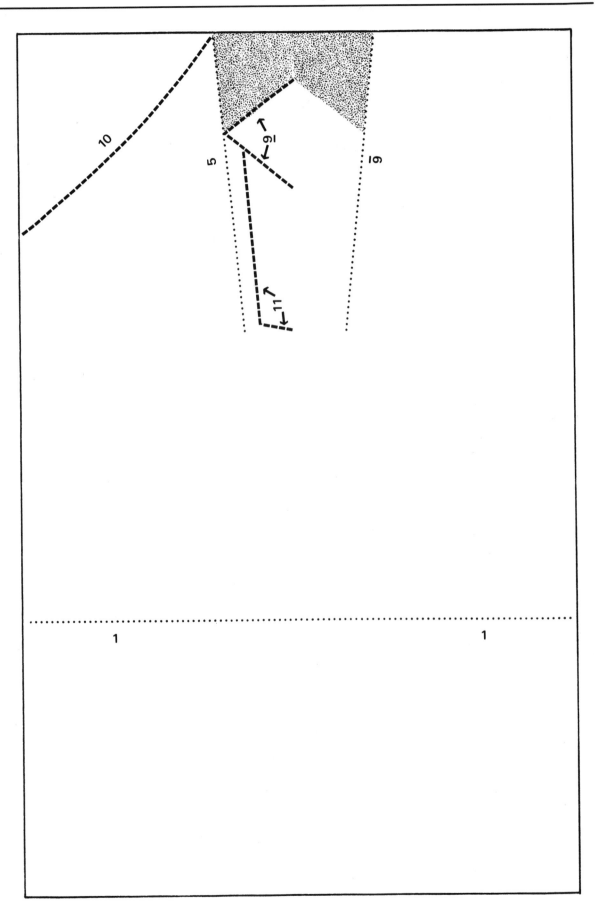

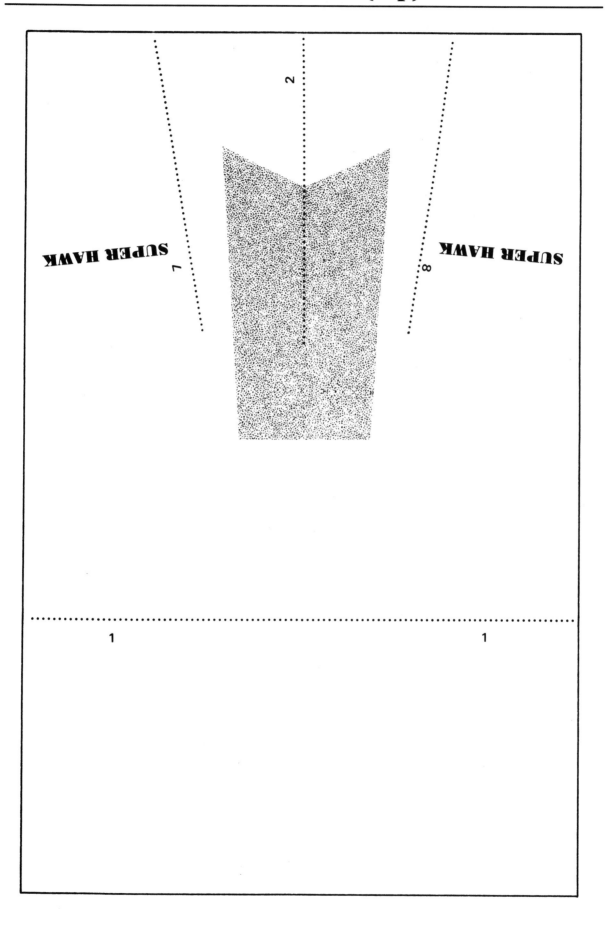

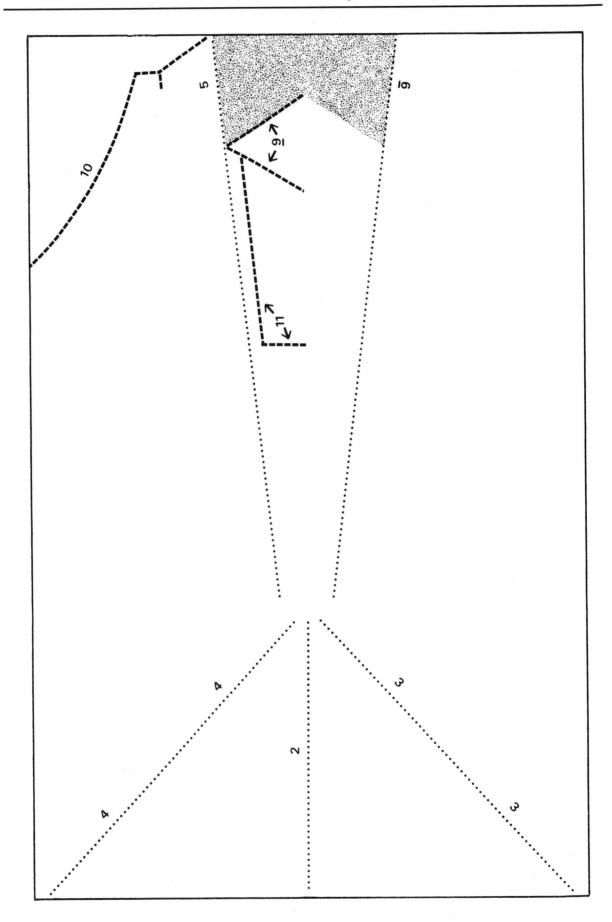

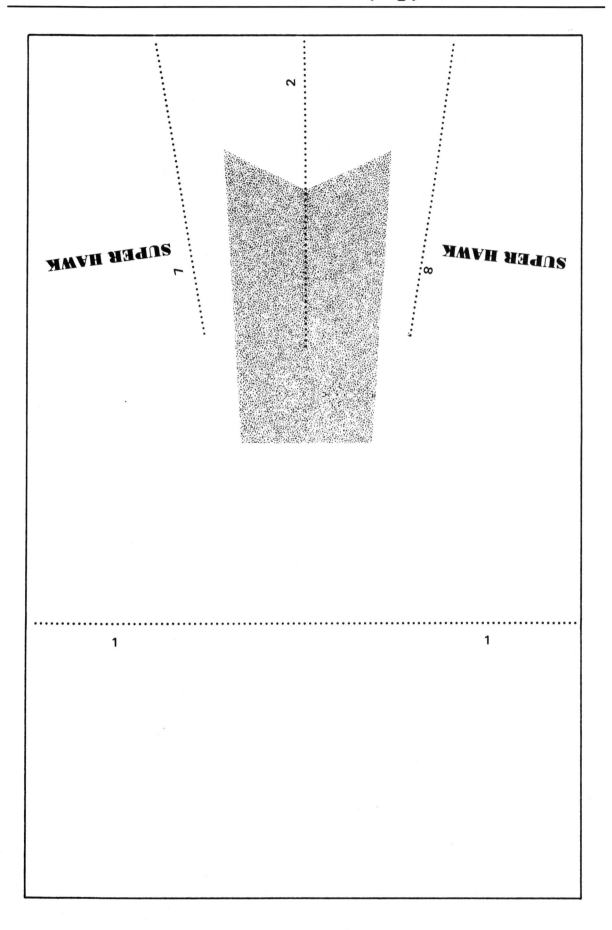

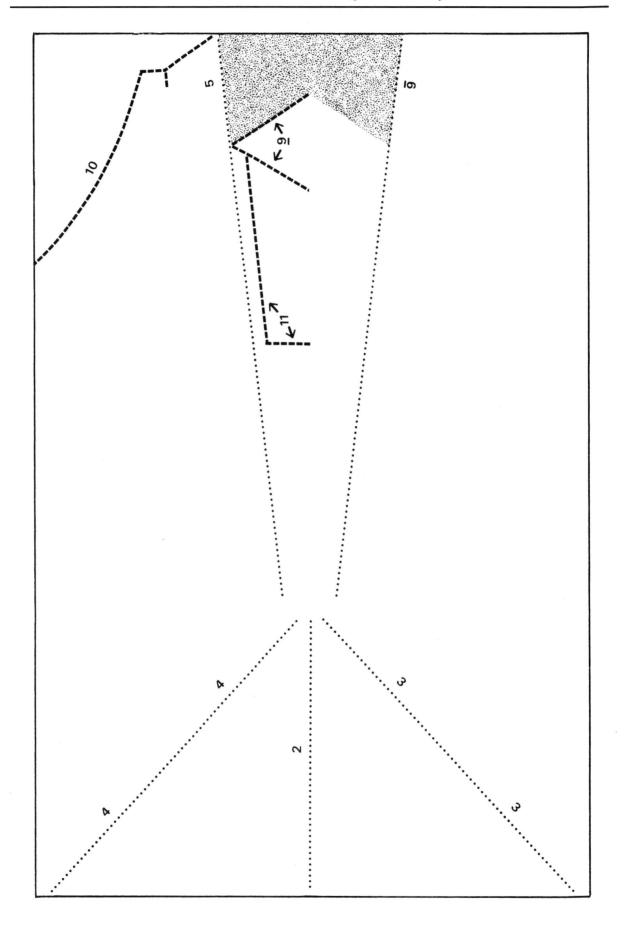

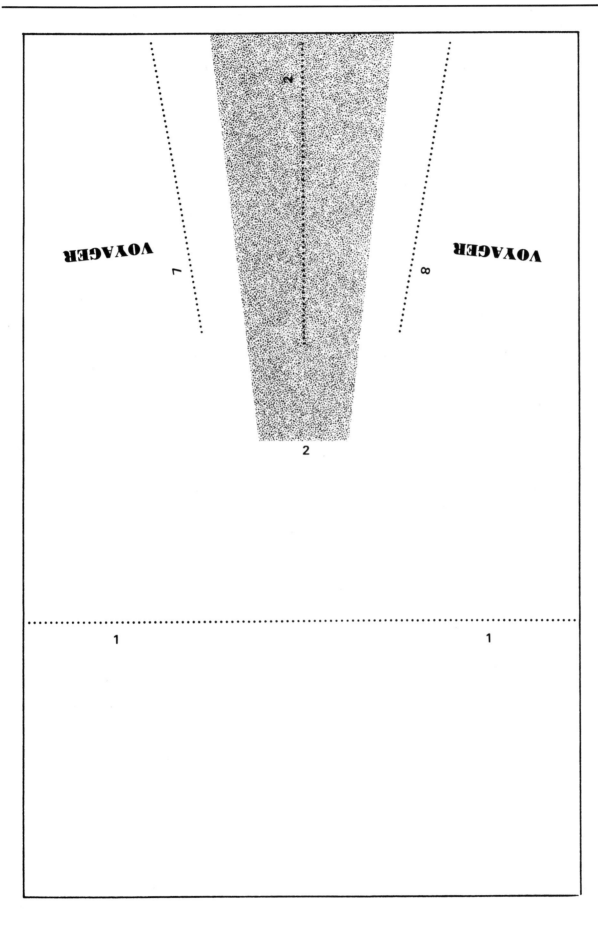

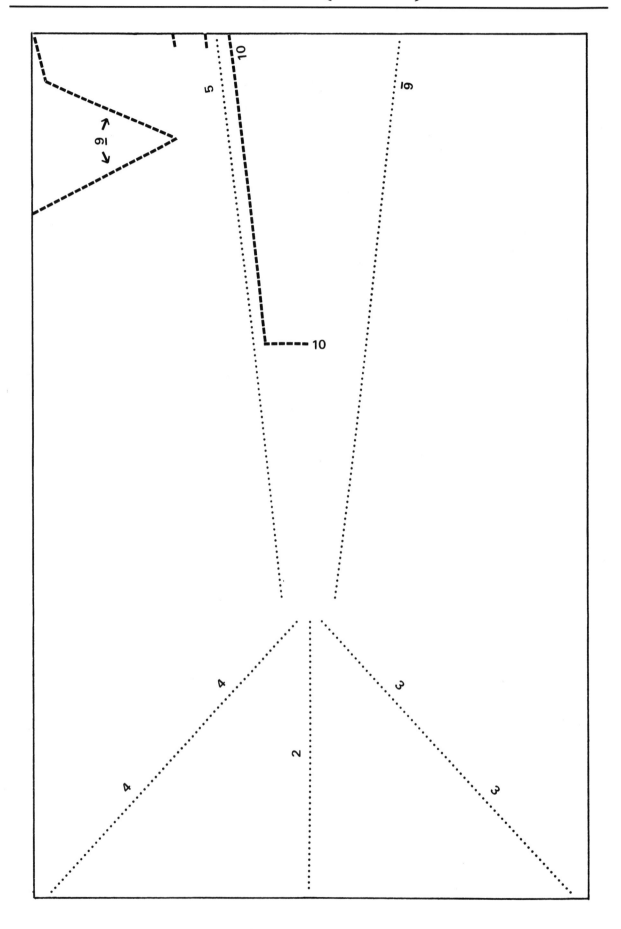

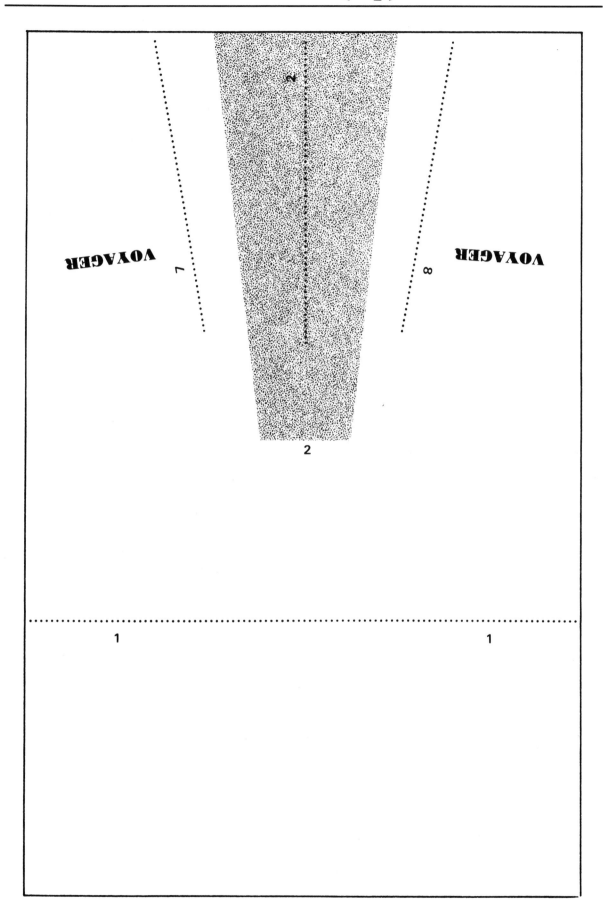

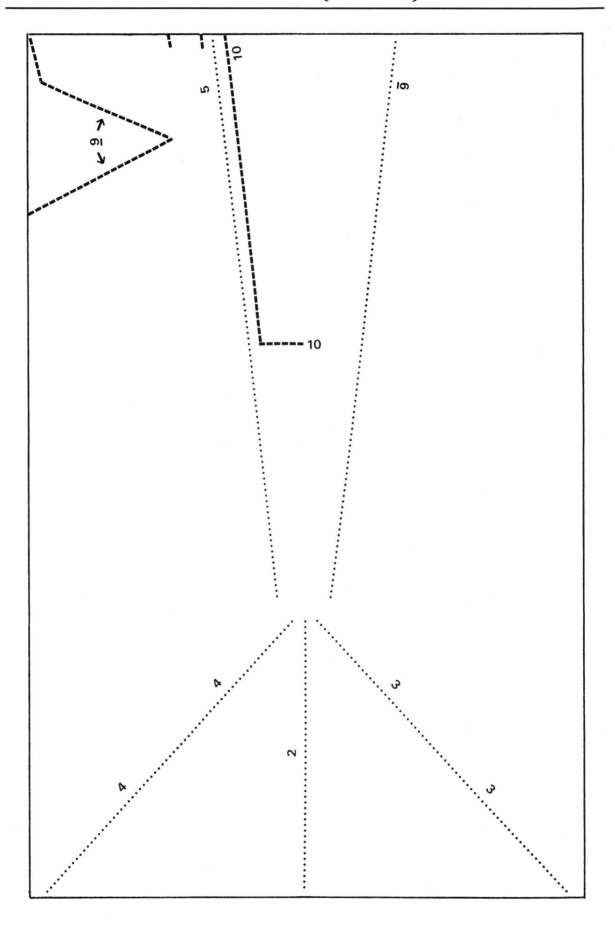

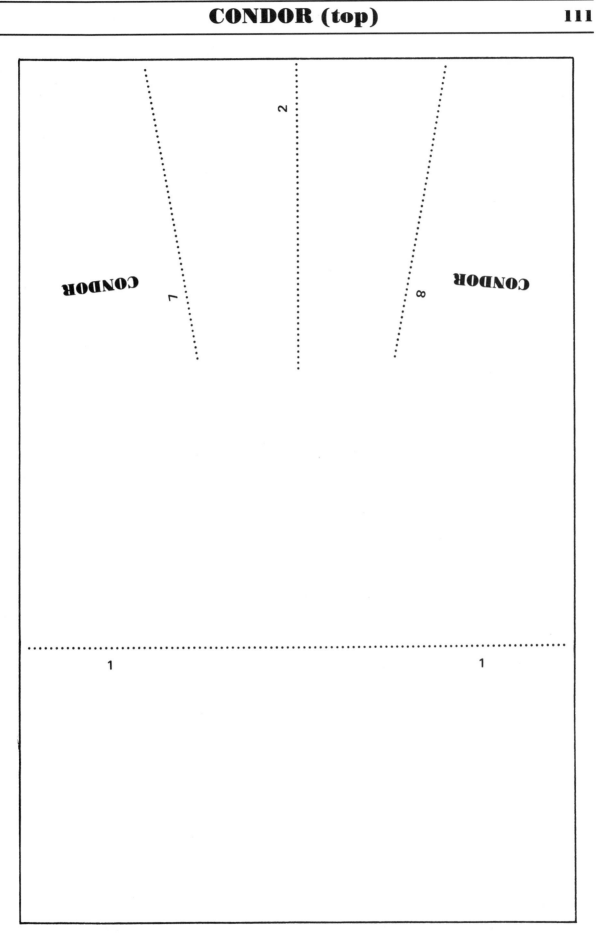

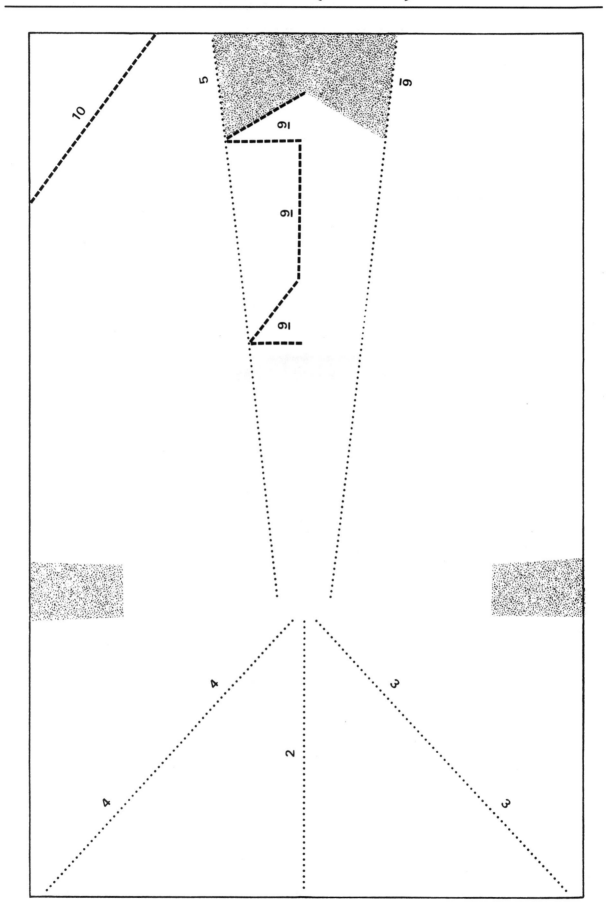

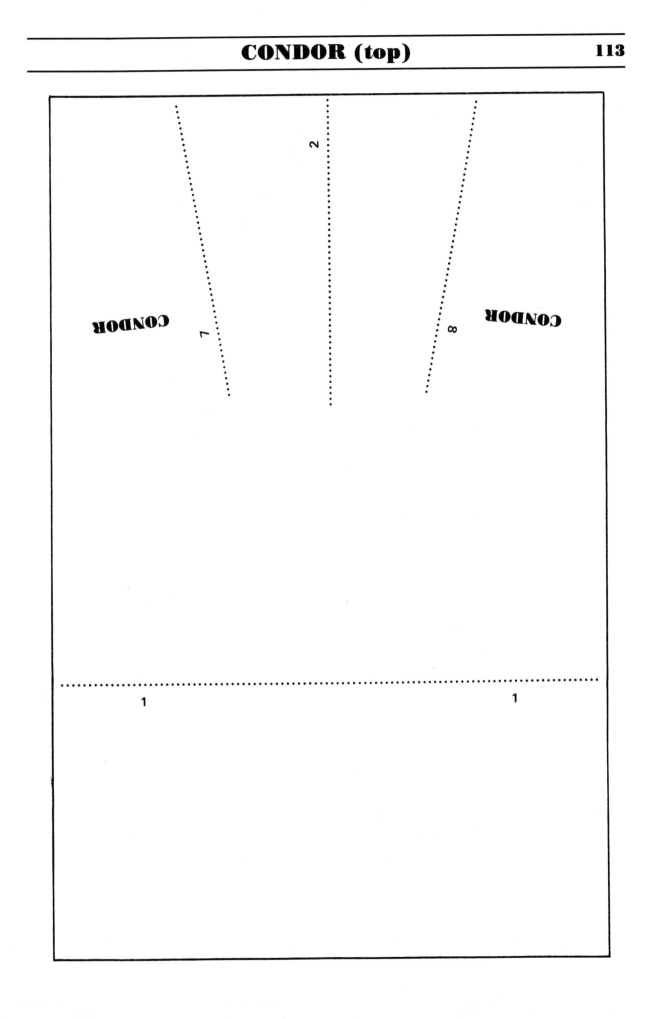

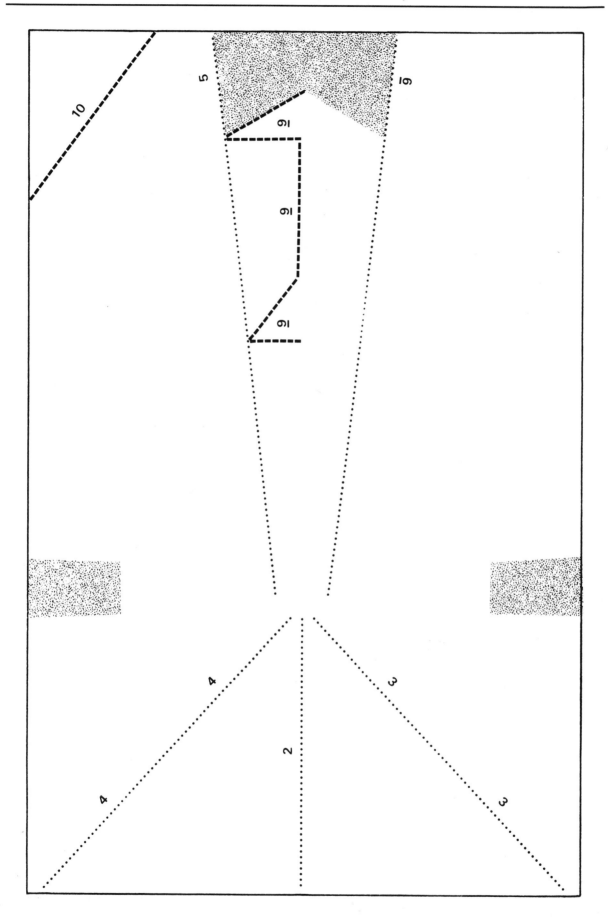

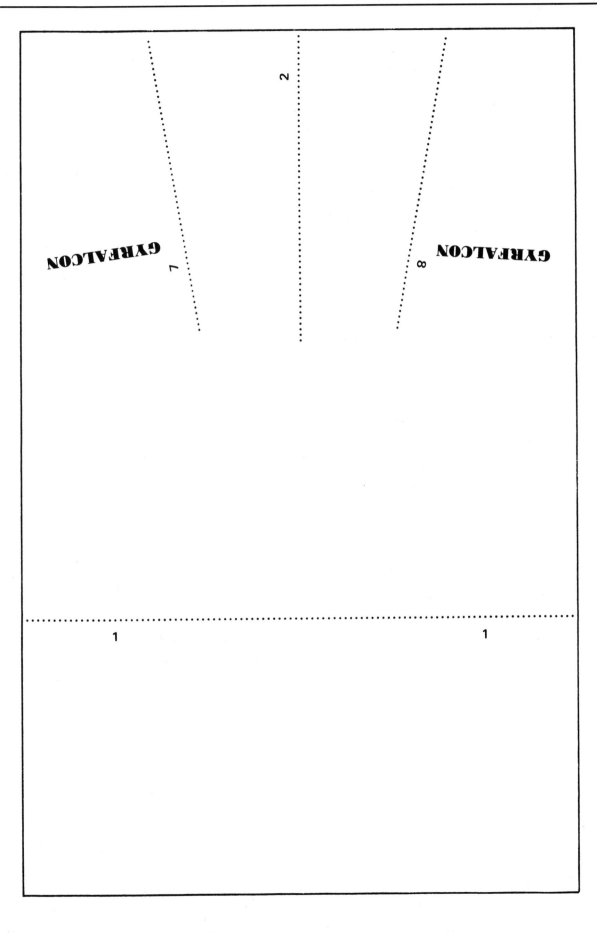

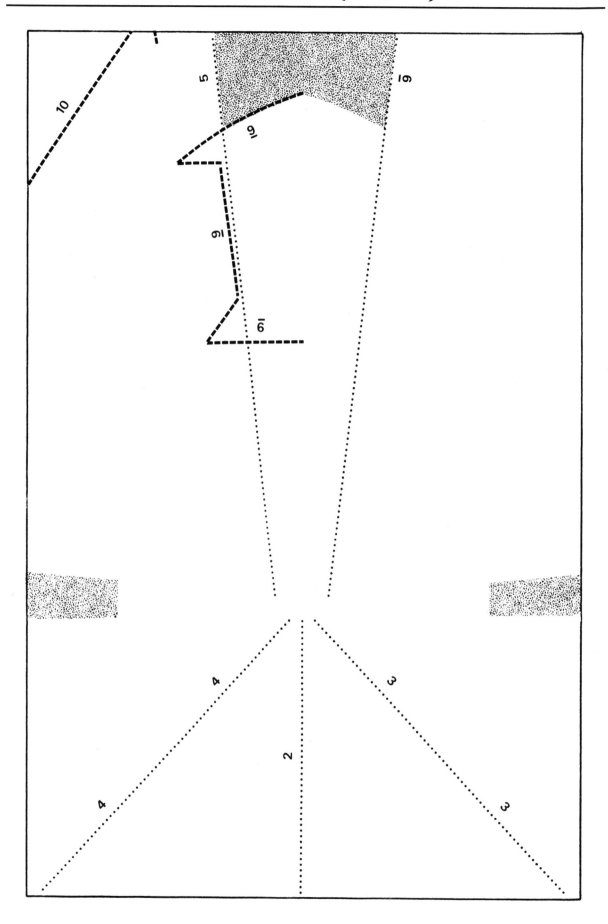

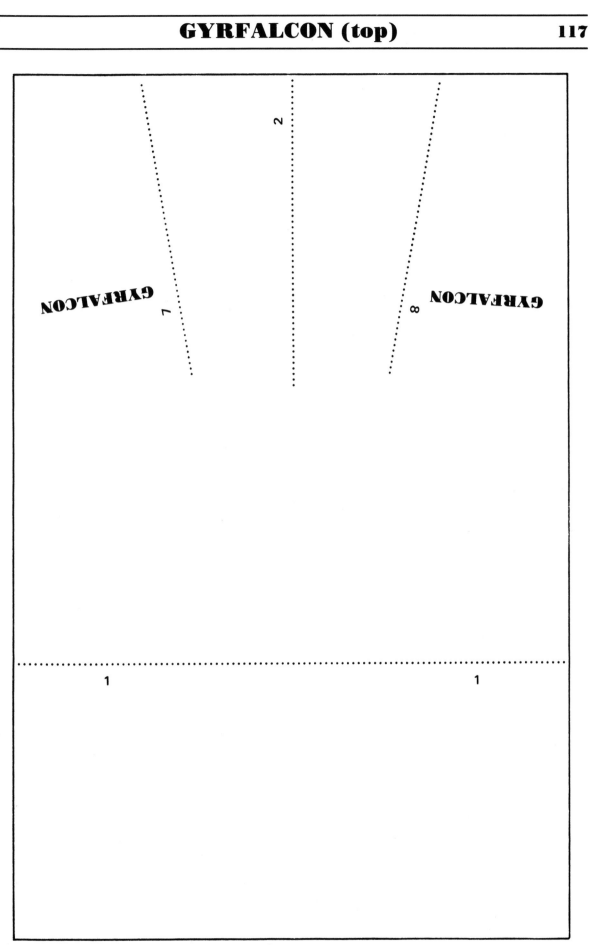

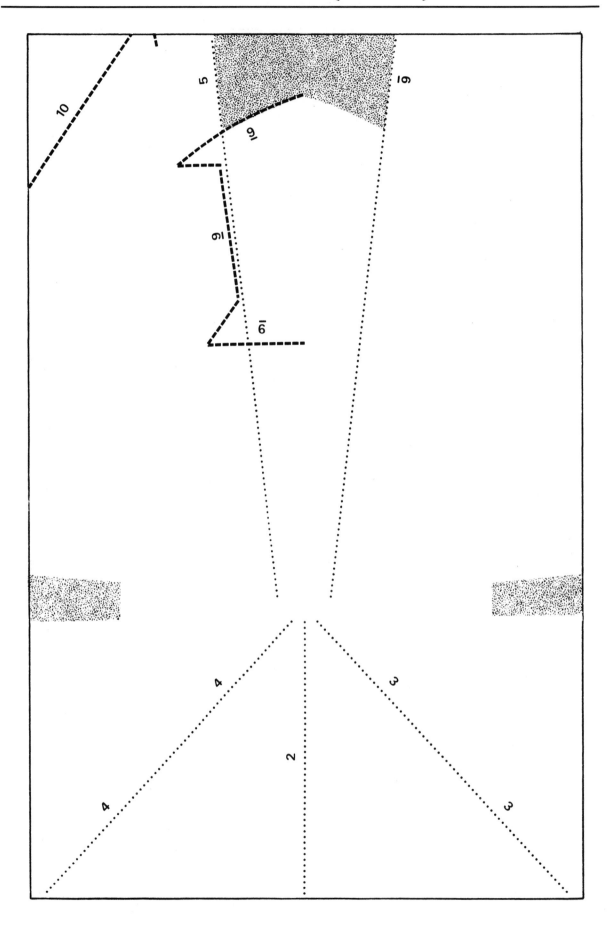

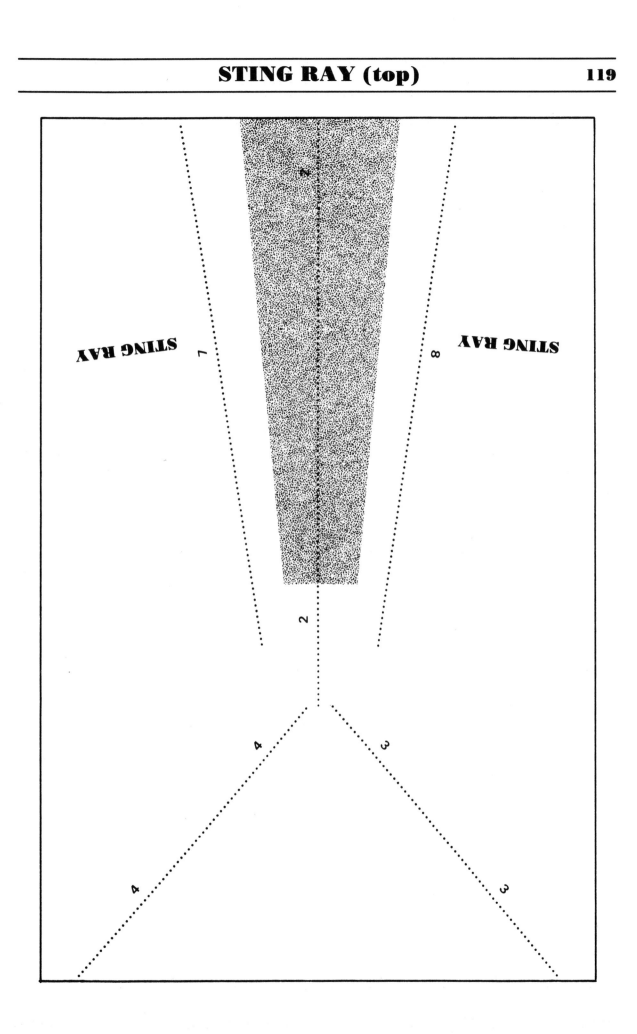

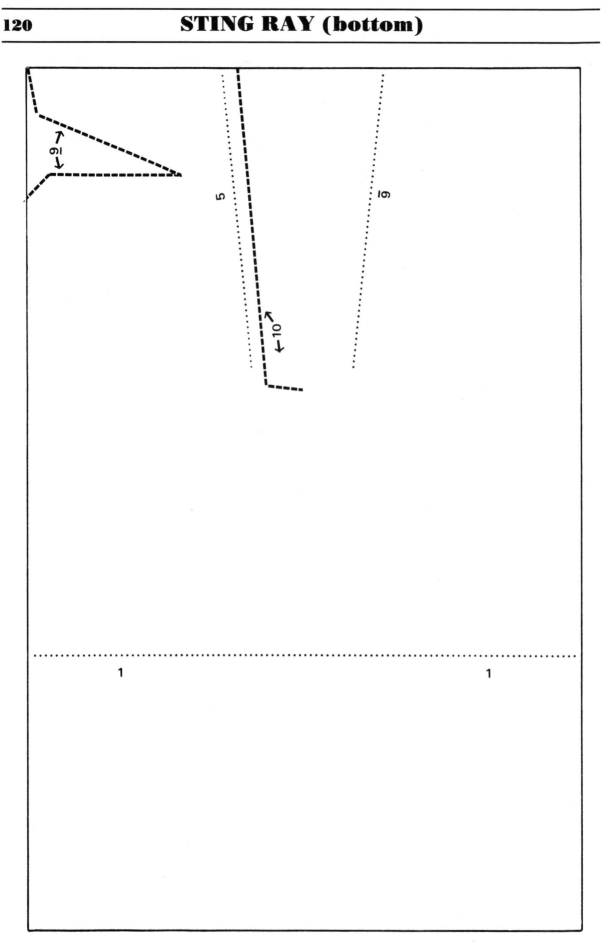

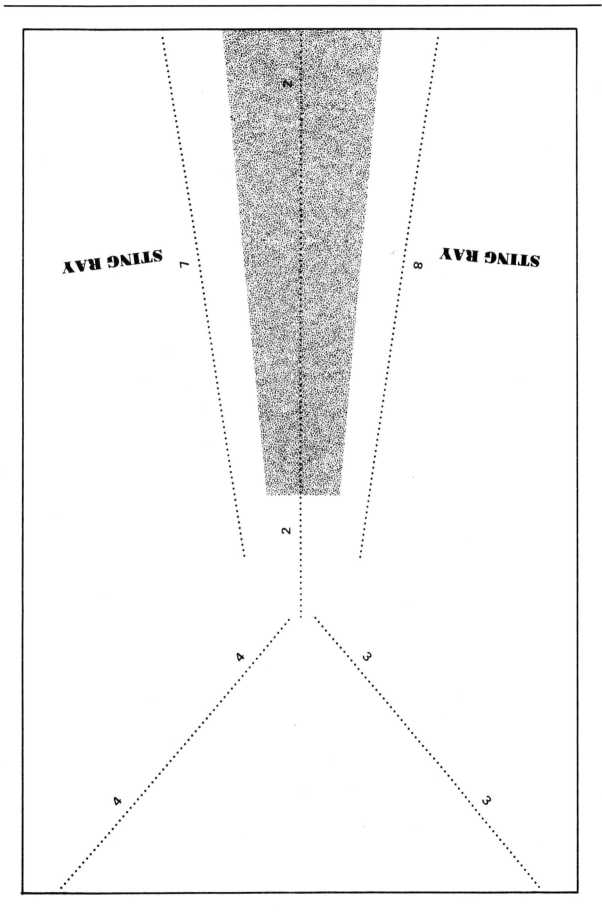

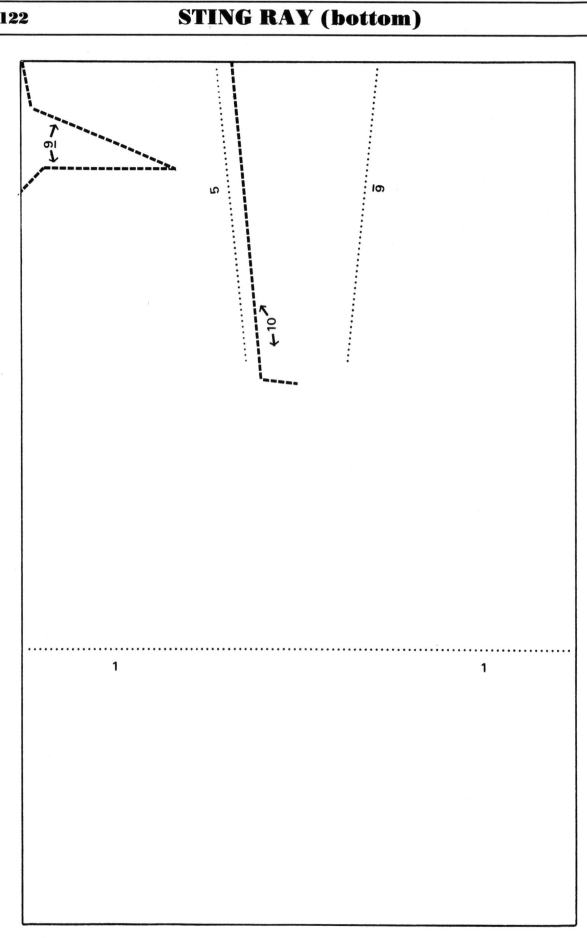

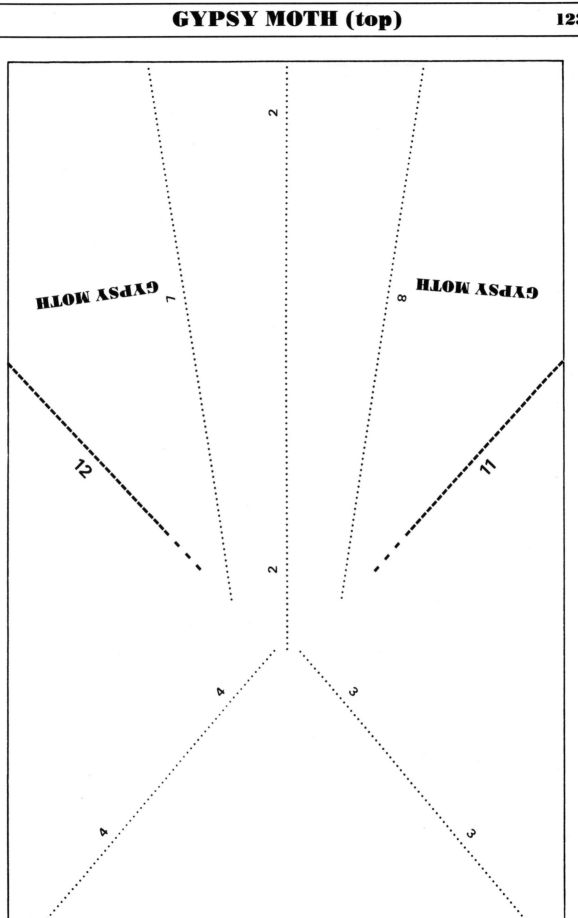

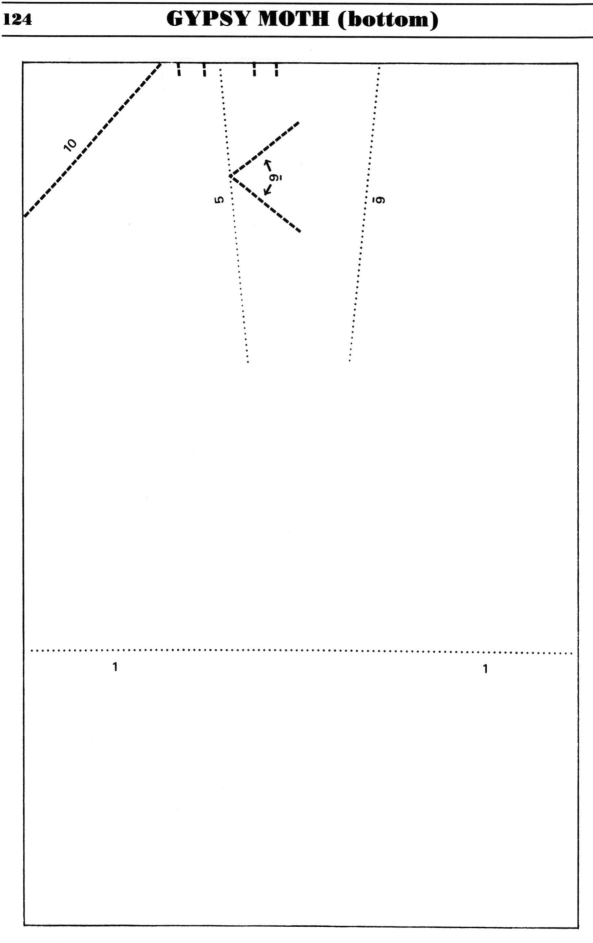

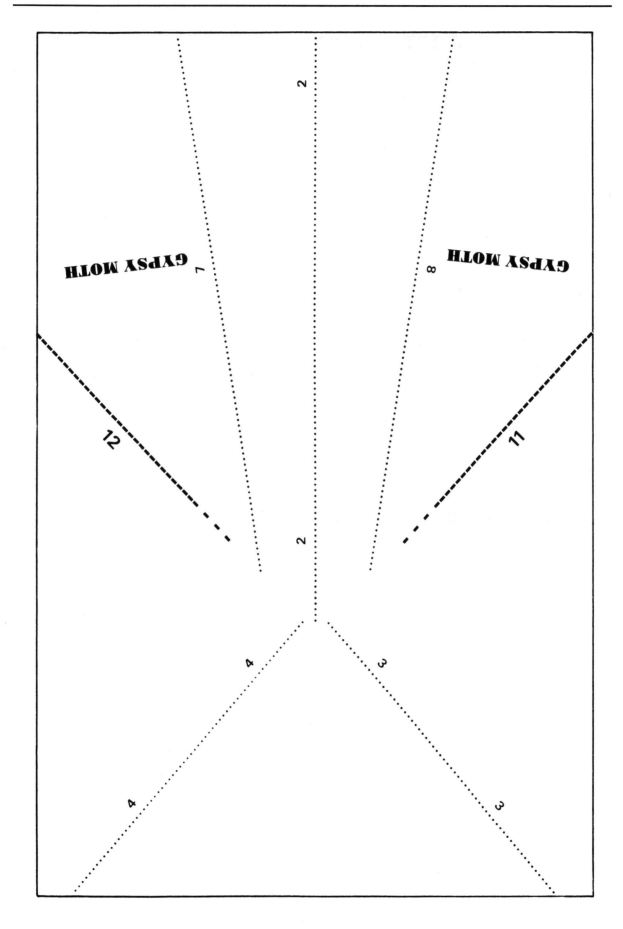

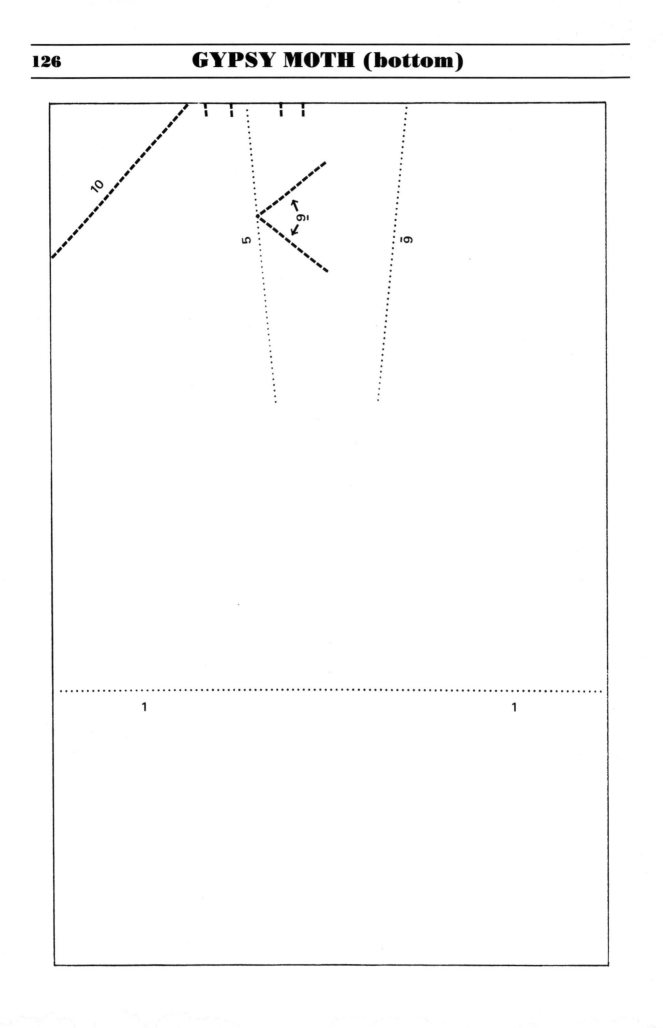